this
Dancing
Ground
of Sky

this Dancing Ground of Sky

THE SELECTED POETRY OF

PEGGY POND CHURCH

Introduction by Shelley Armitage, Ph.D.

R·E·D
CRANE
BOOKS

SANTA FE

First Edition
Manufactured in the United States
Series format by Paulette Livers Lambert
Design by Jim Mafchir
Cover painting by Paulette Livers Lambert

Page ii: Peggy on Pajarito Plateau, New Mexico, ca. 1950s.
Page xiii: Inspiration for the poem "Elegy for the Willow Tree."

Library of Congress Cataloging-in-Publication Data

Church, Peggy Pond
   This dancing ground of sky: the selected poetry of Peggy Pond Church/Peggy Pond Church; introduction by Shelley Armitage.—1st ed.
      p.   cm.
   Includes bibliographical references.
   ISBN 1-878610-28-7
   I. Title.
[PS3505.H946A6   1993]
811'.52--dc20   92-32298
                                                  CIP

Red Crane Books
826 Camino de Monte Rey
Santa Fe, New Mexico 87501

Contents

PART TWO: The Rose, Unfurling

PART THREE: This Dancing Ground of Sky

Preface

Peggy Church often said, "I am a one-book author," referring to *The House at Otowi Bridge*. Yet this statement is not entirely true—many small books of poetry were published from the 1930s through the 1980s. What was true: the published works were pitifully few compared to the prodigious output of a woman who dedicated her life to writing. She wrote daily; if not creating poetry, she recorded the world and her interpretation of it in her many journals. Peggy's work was from her heart, and when it was unappreciated, the criticisms of careless editors broke her. So, in the last years, little was sent to publishers, but much was produced; some of Peggy Pond Church's strongest poems were written in her seventies and early eighties. It was not until the diminishments of age included impaired vision and loss of hearing—catastrophic to one to whom nuances of sound and sight were woven into line and rhythm—that Peggy ended her work, and with it, her life.

She carefully prepared for her death by commissioning representatives to her future. Shelley Armitage was tasked with editing and organizing the many volumes of work that Peggy left behind. I have been assigned as literary executrix. This heavy responsibility has often made me angry. "Here is a voice that must be heard, a talent the world must know! Why didn't she do this herself?" High school English teacher that I am, I hear the echoes of studied poets in Peggy's work—the understanding of nature as in Frost, the precise, sharp-edged images of Amy Lowell, the exact, concise word choices of Emily Dickinson, the use of the specific event to understand the whole in Robinson Jeffers. And yet, she is unique;

she is not a nature poet, yet her life in nature created images and ideas; she is not a woman's poet, to her the woman's condition is part of the human condition. Her voice is very much her own. None who read these poems will be unaffected; some lines will clutch the reader's heart as they do mine. So, my anger has given way to determination; if Peggy could not do this herself, as she truly could not, then we must do it for her. None of us will be sorry.

—*Kathleen Church*

Editor's Foreword

I was lucky enough to meet Peggy Pond Church in Taos in 1986, the last year of her life. I'd asked her to make the trip up to Taos to read her work as part of a summer reading series there. She graciously accepted and now I learn that this was her last public reading. I remember being struck by her warmth, an immediate feeling one could get from her. I was also touched by the fact that her poems were all typed in huge letters. She would flip through several pages of text for even her shorter work. Being curious, I asked to see her manuscript pages, which were covered in abnormally large letters. She laughed with me over these pages, still managing good humor despite her failing eyesight.

Where Peggy Pond Church doesn't fail is in her consistent poetic vision, one that is reflected in the poems you'll read in this collection. The poems you'll find here are organized into three sections that are divided thematically. One central theme of her work is relationship—the self to the self, the self to others, both lovers and friends, men and women. These poems are featured in Part One, "Love's Genius." The middle section, titled "The Rose, Unfurling," features poems that are more social in nature, ones that have more to do with the world outside her private one, and include poems about being a woman and a poet as well as poems that are more mythological in nature. The final section, "This Dancing Ground of Sky," is full of poems that focus on the natural world and the poet's unique vision in relationship to that world.

Each section contains work that is both previously published and unpublished. I have made no distinction between work that has appeared in previously published volumes. A list of such work is included at the end of the book. I felt it was important to make this collection a new one entirely, and felt this was entirely feasible given the large amount of both published and unpublished work available. This collection has an integrity all its own, the overall themes being derived from the work itself, the result being very nearly a conversation with the poet herself.

I'm happy to know that Peggy Pond Church has walked these grounds before all the other contemporary poets of New Mexico. This is challenging territory; what she's managed to do so well is to make this world her own. And to dare to release it when the time came. These poems are ways in which she shaped that world, her gifts to the rest of us here waiting to receive them.

—*Renée Gregorio*

Introduction

When I first met Peggy Pond Church in 1980 in her home on Camino Ranche-ros in Santa Fe, I knew her only by reputation. Although author of the best-selling memoir, *The House at Otowi Bridge*, she was chiefly a poet. "The First Lady of New Mexico poetry, who should be in all poetry collections," W. David Laid wrote in *Books of the South-west*, in his review of *Rustle of Angels*. In 1984, having published her final of eight volumes of poetry, Peggy won the Governor's Award for Literature. Fifty years before, Elizabeth Shepley Sergeant prophesied in *The Saturday Review of Literature* that here was "a pristine young poetess ... probably the first real New Mexican to produce a book of undeniable poetic promise out of her region and her life." The Longmont award, granted for the outstanding merit of *The House at Otowi Bridge*, and the Julia Ellsworth Ford Foundation prize for her humorous children's tale, *The Burro for Angelitos,* certified that a graceful stylist was at work, even in nonfiction. First among the writers published by the Rydal Press in the Writers' Editions during the 1920s and 1930s, Peggy's accomplishments as a poet began along with a flowering of New Mexico arts and letters. Playwright Lanford Wilson, when asked to summarize the best books of 1982 for the *New York Times Book Review*, instead lauded *The House at Otowi Bridge,* which he had just discovered as "one of the most wonderful and surprising books" he'd read in years.

What I didn't know that summer day in 1980, as a represent-
ative from the University of New Mexico I arranged for the gift
of Mrs. Church's papers to the school, was how much I knew of
the poet through her poetry. Years later, at her memorial service
in November, 1986, I was astounded by the variety and number
of people in attendance at St. John's College who had come to
honor her after her death. Her long-time friend, Corina
Santistevan, later noted: "Her friends cut across borders of age,
race, religion, culture, and profession. Young people were at the
services, as well as old men and some friends since childhood,
including an archaeologist, teachers, and librarians. It was a
roomful of a great variety of people who spoke lovingly about
Peggy." Most spoke about her through her poems or memories of
some story associated with them. One young woman told of
working for a tree service, cutting down an old, failing willow
which Peggy later regretted killing and so wrote a poem about it.
In her sadness for the forlorn tree, Peggy hung an old hat on its
few remaining branches. At the Society of Friends' service, the
family distributed a last statement left by the poet which contained
this coda from her "Elegy for a Willow Tree":

Now I, old willow tree from which the birds have fled,
through whose branches the sap no longer rises
leave my own vacancy on the waiting air.

Memories of these aspects of her personality, plus her special
gift for irony and warmth, sifted through the afternoon in quoted
lines, stanzas committed by and to the heart. Somehow the range
of poetry—seventy years of it since she published her first poem
in 1915—and the complexity of life were reflected in the diversity
of the audience. Yet, when contemplating writing her autobiog-
raphy, she recognized the difficulty of assessing either poet or
poetry. (Late in life she was advised by her friend, Lawrence Clark
Powell, professor emeritus at UCLA, to tell her life through the
poetry.) In a letter to May Sarton—one of several in a correspond-
ence that lasted from 1948 to 1986—she remarked that a young

woman had been by that day to look through her files, expressing interest in writing her biography. "But who?" Peggy asked in the letter. "Which poet? Which Peggy?"

The reader of this volume of poems certainly mines a rich and intriguing biography, but also a study subtly drawn, one that contains more than references to the personal life. When asked about her poet's credo, Peggy once replied, "It's the land that wants to be said." She wrote perceptively about the Southwest landscape, not as background or setting but as experienced essence. Love, marriage, family, war, and the woman writer were equally her subjects, yet in each case, as May Sarton observed in another letter to her, she was utterly "controlled, not confessional." Of her *The Ripened Fields: Fifteen Sonnets of a Marriage,* Lawrence Clark Powell noted: "Peggy Pond Church is one of the few poets to grace the Southwest—I mean poets, not versifiers with which the region abounds. Her emotions are deep, her language controlled. She sees the landscape with the far sight of history and also with the preciseness of a knowing observer of the nearby."

Hers is a story as rich as the history of New Mexico itself, the poetry sophisticated because of its experiential and universal appeal. "Sensory, yet celestial" Peggy called the achievement of fellow New Mexico poet, Haniel Long; her life and consequent art also has that kind of resonance. Born December 1, 1903 in Watrous, New Mexico, then the territory of New Mexico at the locale known as Valmora, she represented the fourth generation of her family to feel the pull of the earth. Peggy not only marks the early Watrous flood as significant in her young life, but remembers that the search for place was continuous. In the 13 years from kindergarten through high school, she attended several different schools, never more than two years in any one of them. But growing up summers on the Pajarito Plateau, the outdoor life— the beauty of the canyons and mountains, the mysteries of the Anasazi Indians—permanently influenced the precocious, yet shy, girl. The opportunity for free and independent discovery, riding horseback, hiking, or observing the evidence of ancient societies, influenced Church's solitary, almost transcendental, love of nature and offered a rare chance for her to experience the wilderness in ways most girls of that period could not. In the winter of 1917–1918, she attended Santa Fe High School, her only year of schooling in New Mexico, except for six months at a convent in Albuquerque when she was eight. Guided by a governess at ages eleven and twelve, she learned the names of wildflowers and mesas and began to feel a love for poetry. Her mother also recited aloud to the children, particularly from the *Child's Garden of Verses* and Kipling's *The Ballad of East and West*. Her first poem was published by *St. Nicholas* magazine when she was still in her teens. In high school at Hillside School in Connecticut, she won an *Atlantic Magazine* prize of $50 for a poem. She spent two years at Smith College beginning in 1922, leaving in 1924 to marry Fermor Church, a young man from Washington, Connecticut who had come out to teach at the Los Alamos Ranch School. As the first faculty wife at the school, Peggy found the isolated mesas anything but dull. Tracing the myriad "roads to utterness," far from the tyranny of the clock, telephone, or even the calendar, she wrote poetry throughout these years at the school where the Churches reared three boys. In 1943, the school was commandeered by the federal government for the Manhattan Project and the development of the atomic bomb.

During the early 1930s, Peggy became interested in Jungian analysis. During this time she studied her dreams and began a kind of introspection that lasted, as reflected in a series of journals, throughout most of her life. After her two initial books of poems (from which several of the poems originally appeared in the *Atlantic*, *Poetry*, and *Saturday Review*), Peggy's reflectiveness led to a much different voice in her third volume of poems, *Ultimatum for Man*. The family moved to Taos in 1943, and in this book Peggy examines the consequences of war and destruction juxtaposed against personal lives. In 1948, she became a member of the Society of Friends, attended meetings, and published in the Quaker journal, *Inward Light*. Her interest in the psychological continued at Berkeley, where Ferm lived in 1956. During this period, Peggy also wrote *The House at Otowi Bridge*, beginning the memoir after Edith Warner's death in 1951. *The Ripened Fields*, sonnets on her marriage, was published 1957 and demonstrated many of the personal concerns the poet experienced in regard to that relationship.

After moving back to Santa Fe in 1960, the couple remained involved in the life of the city as well as in the rich area of life they particularly shared together—their hikes, retreats, and drives through the heart of New Mexico and the Southwest. Peggy began research on Mary Austin, another famous Santa Fe resident whom she had briefly known in the early 1930s. She attended lectures at St. John's College by John Holt, Robert Bly, and Joseph Campbell, as well as seminars on Pablo Neruda, Whitman, Thoreau, and Yeats. In 1975, Ferm died of a brain tumor. After this loss, Peggy brought out *New and Selected Poems* in 1976, *The Lament at Tsankawi Mesa* in 1980, *Rustle of Angels* in 1981, and her final volume, *Birds of Daybreak*, in 1985. She continued her correspondences with poets May Sarton and Denise Levertov, editor Roland Dickey (who had published *The House at Otowi Bridge*), Lawrence Clark Powell, and her Taos friend, Corina Santistevan. Shortly before her death, she began close scrutiny of her journals (some she had burned in the 1930s). What remained were rearranged in collections called "The Terminal Journal" (about the death of her husband), "Pajarito" (nature writings), "Poli" (the record of her relationship to her dog), and daily journals kept since the 1950s. While attending seminars on Greek tragedy as well as lectures at St. John's, she continued her intense musical interests and reading, was interviewed for radio programs and magazines, and honored with autograph parties and awards. On October 23, 1986, she took her own life according to the precepts of the Hemlock Society, of which she was a member.

Though Church maintained throughout her life that she was not a "member" of the Santa Fe writers' group which achieved some renown during the 1920s and 1930s, she nevertheless read at the "Poets' Roundups" and knew members of this group, including Alice Corbin Henderson, Mary Austin, and Haniel Long. There is at least an implied influence and place for her among these older writers who established a kind of writers' colony in New Mexico. Despite New Mexico's rich Spanish and Mexican literary tradition, when the first influx of Anglo writers to Santa Fe and Taos began, artists such as Mary Austin bemoaned the lack of a wider audience and more conscious recognition of New Mexico's native literary sources. "One confidently predicts here," she wrote, "the rise, within appreciable time, of the next great and fructifying world culture." Another émigré, author, archaelogist, historian, and journalist, Charles F. Lummis, rhapsodized about the Southwest in the opening paragraph of *The Land of Poco Tiempo*: "Sun, silence, and adobe—that is New Mexico in three words. . . . It is the Great American Mystery—the National Rip Van Winkle—the United States which is *not* the United States." Harriet Monroe, editor of the little Chicago magazine, *Poetry*, continued this line: "Why go to Greece or China? This Southwest, which is but one chapter of our rich tradition, is our own authentic wonderland— a treasure-trove of romantic myth—profoundly beautiful and significant, guarded by ancient races practicing their ancient rites, in a region of incredible color and startling natural grandeur."

More recently, Robert Coles in his *Eskimos, Chicanos, Indians* offered a somewhat more scientific explanation for this same response: "At the altitude of high northern New Mexico, the air has lost one-fourth its weight; it is low in carbon dioxide and oxygen and has therefore also lost its capacity to refract or diffuse light." But even the social scientist waxed poetic: "The hazy, somewhat softened, even blurred vision of the coastal plains or the prairie gives way to a clear, bright, almost harsh, sometimes blinding field of view. Air that an outsider has come to regard as transparent suddenly becomes transluscent—so sharp, so clean, so light that one feels in a new world possessed of new eyes." Indeed, for the Anglo newcomers of the 1920s and 1930s, exotic, light-charged New Mexico was a spiritual place of new vision. Embracing this place and its multicultural heritage as their lost roots in a depersonalized America, they created a body of work containing folk materials and professing a literary potential. Moreover, many of these newcomers had the sophistication and training to tap these resources. Working as editors and collectors, with connections to the eastern establishment, they attracted other famous writers and artists to come to the Southwest, including Carl Sandburg, Vachel Lindsay, Witter Bynner, and Ezra Pound. In 1928, Alice Corbin Henderson, assistant to Harriet Monroe at *Poetry* magazine, edited *The Turquoise Trail: An Anthology of New Mexico Poetry*, which included Peggy Pond Church along with thirty other poets. Among them were Mary Austin, Witter Bynner, Paul Horgan, Spud Johnson, D.H. Lawrence, Haniel Long, Mabel Dodge Luhan, and Eugene Manlove Rhodes. With the advent of the "Poets' Roundups," supported by Alice Corbin, Peggy, Witter Bynner, and Haniel Long, public readings and publications through the Writers' Editions gave voice to a body of poetry along with the growing publication of translations, novels, and literary and social science journals. By the end of the 1930s, a sixteen-page "Southwest Book List for 1938-1939" named eighty-eight writers "living in and about Santa Fe," with 280 adult and juvenile titles that they had produced, in which Church was included. The ultimate purpose of the Writers' Editions, "a cooperative group of writers living in the Southwest," was to see that "regional publication would foster the growth of American literature."

Along with the discovery of the Southwest as an exotic, art-inspiring region, often romanticized, writer Erna Fergusson noted that it was also a testing ground, a hard country, forbidding and challenging. She writes in *Our Southwest*:

> The arid Southwest has always been too strong, too indominable for most people. Those who can stand it have had to learn that man does not modify this country; it transforms him, deeply. . . . It is wilderness where a man may get back to the essentials of being a man. It is magnificence forever rewarding to a man courageous enough to seek to renew his soul.

Indeed, rather than particularized as uniquely regional in its folklore, geography, and ancient history and peoples, this Southwest possessed, in common with all dynamic places of the heart, qualities both local and universal. In their assessment of the effect of this landscape on literature in *Southwest Heritage*, literary historians T.M. Pearce and Mabel Major noted two themes that have emerged from this territory:

> The recurring motif in the poetry of the Southwest is the timelessness of Nature, the antiquity of the Indian and Spanish civilization of the region, and the recentness of the white man in this old land, together with the briefness of the individual life. The poet looks at a rock covered with inscriptions, a piece of ancient pottery, the dim painting of hands in a cave, a circle of trees where a house has been and no house is, an age-old road, and writes of the twin deities, Permanence and Evanescence.

Experiencing directly these themes, as well as the individual's quest for spiritual growth, Peggy Church embraced the Southwest's noted extremes, experiencing the cycles of flowering, drought, and migration that have left us Chaco, Mesa Verde, and Hovenweep. Primal experiences of flood and drought are key to her life. Moreover, she grew up in a landscape but was dispossessed of it—she lost that which had succored her childhood and young womanhood. During one of the particularly challenging periods in her life—1932–1934—after losing her father to brain cancer, suffering a schism in her marriage, and confusions about her own destiny, mentor and poet-friend Haniel Long encouraged her to focus on poetry. The act of writing not only renewed her creative, positive life, but reconnected her as maker of metaphors, symbols, and parables, with the cycles of self. Writing in 1985 the "Afterword" to Long's prose poem, *The Interlinear of Cabeza de Vaca* (originally published in 1936), she linked the meaning of the poem to the poet's development in the landscape. Like the Spanish explorer, who through deprivation and hardship came to know himself and his fellows by "shedding his skin," so Long discovered in himself the ability to feel for others. She writes:

Without straying in any important detail from the historical account, Long makes the matter-of-fact Spanish soldier's journey an adventure of inner transformation, an adventure in the invisible realm of the human soul. "What can describe a happening in the shadows of the soul?" his Cabeza de Vaca wonders at the beginning of the *Interlinear*. What Haniel saw in the rugged Spanish soldier was, I am convinced, a reflection of his own inner journey. He was a poet who took the soul seriously in the same way Keats did who called the world "a vale of soul-making," and once wrote, "I began by seeing how man was formed by circumstances—and what are circumstances?—but the touchstones of his heart?—and what are touchstones?—but the provings of his heart?—and what are provings of the heart but fortifiers or alterers of his own nature?—and what is his altered nature but his Soul?"

Nature and one's nature for Church are intimately bound. As she revealed in her assessment of how the role of the poet relates to themes and images in Long's poem, the choice of such native, folkloristic subjects is an act of autobiography, containing within it elements of an older history—archetypal, primordial events in the "place" of the self. She notes that Long, like his Cabeza de Vaca, had his own shipwreck—a breakdown, a descent into the darkness of self—which necessitated his relating in a new way to others. Noting that Keats, whom Long read, also wrote about the poetic nature, she maintains what brought Long out of his black period was "losing himself in another human being and thus becoming aware that there is something in all of us, not the combative and possessive ego, through which we are able to share life and wholeness with another." She explains:

> It seems to me that the *Interlinear of Cabeza de Vaca* might be a portion of Haniel Long's autobiography, an account of transformations that had taken place in his own journey through the vale of soul-making. He has recreated Cabeza de Vaca in his own image. It is the image of the poet who

has emerged from the wilderness of self with an understanding of the Invisible not learned from books or teachers but from the provings of the heart.

The same observations may be made about Church's poetry. While she writes often directly from experience, with awe and zeal, in an effort to hone the beauty of the moment or to apply it to some corresponding personal awareness, her focus on particulars of the land and people results in an ecstatic attention, at once holistic. Another "regional" writer, Eudora Welty, describes how place animates the writer's philosophy and style:

It may be that place can focus the gigantic, voracious eye of genius and bring its gaze to point. Focus then means awareness, discernment, order, clarity, insight—they are like the attributes of love. The act of focusing itself has beauty and meaning; it is the act that continued in, turns into meditation, into poetry. . . the question of place resolves itself into the point of view.

Losing oneself in this love for the landscape also makes for new discoveries. Place and poetics in Church's work are significantly linked. She began the habit of writing as an exorcism of her shy self when she was a girl, and this habit took shape in the beating out with her fingers on a tabletop formal rhythms of poems she had read and heard. From these more formal constructions, we see her moving to experimentations with controlled free verse, more "natural" rhythms. She has said that it is chiefly sound that gives birth and then meaning to a poem, that a "poetic ear" is key. "I had a good ear for it. I heard it and read it out loud. Before radio and television and movies, what we had was the drama of the landscape." When asked how, specifically, this drama affected her voice, tone, and meaning, she added, "I have listened endlessly to the Rio de los Frijoles." Likewise, Church read a number of poets for their language, the way in which sound makes meaning. She was influenced by her study of Blake, Yeats, Eliot, Rilke, Neruda,

Thoreau, and Wordsworth. Her formal education in poetics reflects a poetry whose meaning is shaped by landscape. Reading Neruda and Rilke in their original Spanish and German, she commented that she took greatest note of words that defied translation, whose sounds in their native tongue remained key. Thus, form for her became a matter of response, at once mysterious, even evanescent, yet permanently shaped. After the Manhattan Project, she commented that to make sense of her uprootings and the larger questions of world safety, harmony, and peace, she "looked for patterns." In her poems, which treat the ideas of universal community, the sanctity of sacred places, even the poet's aging ("like a shipwreck," she once called it), her own homing pattern is evident: "I write to keep things from getting lost," she said.

Another key to Church's ability to write personally, yet universally, is her gender and her attitudes about the woman artist. Lawrence Clark Powell recognized in *The Ripened Fields* "a finer distillation" than Meredith's *Modern Love* because she had a "woman's sensitivity. . . rather than bitter, at last accepting and serene." He continued in his assessment to note that this quality helped assure her "a place in our literature beyond the regional." Typically, the conflicts for the woman who is writer have been thought to create a schism within the self—a disjunctive position between societal expectations and personal desire that often contributes to anything but the "accepting and serene." Church, though never really a careerist, experienced many of the contrarieties of being a creative woman. Adrienne Rich (in *Adrienne Rich's Poetry*) writes insightfully about the conflicts between the ego necessary to creativity and the traditional expectations of womanhood:

> For a poem to coalesce, for a character or action to take
> shape, there has to be an imaginative transformation of
> reality which is in no way passive. And a certain freedom of
> mind is needed—freedom to press on, to enter the currents
> of your thought as a glider pilot, knowing that your motion

can be sustained, that the buoyancy of your attention will not be suddenly snatched away. Moreover, if the imagination is to transcend and transform experience it has to question, to challenge, to conceive of alternative, perhaps to the very life you are living at the moment. . . . So often to fulfill being a female being by trying to fulfill traditional female functions in a traditional way is in direct conflict with the subversive function of the imagination.

Rich sees a direct conflict between love—how it is tradition-ally defined by culture—and the ego necessary for creativity, achievement, and ambition, which often is at the expense of others. Likewise, May Sarton sees the conflict similarly within the woman artist, "who becomes one at her own peril." Sarton explains that the conflict is between the central value of relationship which puts her at odds with the necessary ego, the imagination:

I think where it is harder to be a woman is when the woman is also an artist and thus torn apart between life and art in a way that men are simply not. A young man goes to college and goes into a career and marries right on the trajectory he has designed in college. The young woman who wants to write, say, and goes to college and then marries, if she has children, for about ten years or more suddenly is thrown back into a life of domesticity where most of her energy must go into the home. The artist is buried. . . . Personal relations do not eat at men in the same way, it seems to me. They are not primarily nurturers and women, even single women, are.

In her nonfiction studies of the lives of two creative women— Edith Warner in *The House at Otowi Bridge* and Mary Austin in *Wind's Trail*—Church indirectly mused about this creative di-lemma as she also thematically reflected her personal struggles with it in some of the poems. In Warner, she saw the ability to unite the seemingly disparate, to link lives significantly together through the wells of "woman's wisdom," gentleness, and sensitivity, even to face death serenely. On the other hand, Church believed that ultimately Mary Austin gave over her own woman's self to an omnivorous ego—through sacrificing her tenderness, which granted perception, deep feeling, and a love of the landscape. For Church, then, ego and imagination are not synonymous. Rather, she advocates that women, as connected as they are to primal sources, have a unique wisdom to bridge the outer and inner worlds, rather than suffer what is traditionally viewed as conflict. As she wrote of Long's loss of ego as necessary for his transformation as a man and poet, so she champions woman's "natural" ability to be reborn in the "loss" of self. In "Lines for a Woman Poet," written for May Sarton, she first admires the woman poet, riding like a falconer into battle with the singing bird on her shoulder:

> *I know that bird. I know that falcon eye,*
> *those beating wings that drive it toward the sun,*
> *the whirling plunge of light and the curved beak*
> *and how it tears the heart to drink the blood,*
> *the living blood on which its song must feed.*

She continues by acknowledging the "god's indifference to our mortal pain," naming the throes of Daphne and Leda. She says:

> *We cannot soar*
> *like birds toward the sun. We must endure*
> *the weight of winter and the darkened moon,*
> *not like Van Gogh who was devoured by light*
> *until his brush bled fire.*

But far from the mere, simplistic, silent suffering in order to make the poem, is the woman's own unique strength, her ability to relate, connect, save, and unite, beyond the egoistic approach:

> *Let the fierce phoenix go with his sharp cry*
> *toward the flaming sun, oh mythical bird*
> *that would consume your heart. Lie down, lie down*

now among roots and leaves and let your eyes
be dark as the closed child's and let the mole
speak his blind wisdom to your folded hand.
Birth is not had by willing. Let the rose
unfurl, in time like air, what summer knows.

Unwilling to reduce the mysteries of the woman artist or the self to the classic babies-or-books argument, Church also does not see the birthing image of the poem here as a "passive" motherhood. She is perhaps closer to Rilke in her assessment of the wells of creativity and how they relate to being a woman when she quotes him in her journals, "I await the birth hour of a new clarity," which is Rilke's line about the coming of the muse. Church sees the muse as an androgynous source. In an exchange of letters on this matter with May Sarton, she says the muse is like an "electric current," an "epiphany" sparked by person, event, or thing, and that when he has been male, she later realized he was but "an incarnation of the inner being." Influenced by Jungian thought, Church ultimately related creativity to the striving for balance between the male and female parts of the self. The uniqueness of being a woman artist, however, was the ability to seize upon the poem as an act of relatedness and relationship rather than lone ego. Even the con-flicts—her quoting of Yeats, for instance, "the quarrel with our-selves makes poetry"—she thought essential to tenderness and nurturing. Whether geological or psychological, Church's poems most often unite the inner and outer worlds as well as the parts of the self: "I realize the important things to me have been the epiphanies. . . . Usually, for me, things seen, rather than things done. I have never forgotten—I must have been between five and six—a brilliant cowslip growing at the center of a bog in a cow pasture, my longing to approach it, barefoot as I was, but not daring for fear I'd be sucked down into the bog. But the cowslip is still there, inside. Decades later, reading *The Secret of the Golden Flower*, I was reminded."

Reading Church's poetry, one cannot ignore the primal quality of the dominant image, event, or experience. Much like the imagist group of poets she tangentially was acquainted with in New Mexico (the work of Pound, Corbin Henderson, and Harriet Monroe), meaning in Church's poems often begins with the values of rhythm and tone as connected to the image. Form then arises from the poet's meditative awareness of values in the world and within. Rather than a documentary realism, however, Church accomplishes through the image a *translation* of experience— indeed the value of that experience that imparts a keener sense of being alive. Proust advocated in *The Past Recaptured* that it is underneath these little recorded details—images, say, of nature, domestic life, a marriage—that reality is hidden:

> . . . the grandeur in the distant sound of an airplane or in the lines of the spires of St. Hilaire, the past contained in the savor of a madeline . . . they have no meaning if one does not extract it from them. . . . The grandeur of real art is to rediscover, grasp again, and lay before us that reality from which we become more and more separated as the formal knowledge which we substitute for it grows in thickness and imperviousness—that reality which there is grave danger we might die without having known and yet which is simply our life.

For Church, this translation from the simple image, keenly observed, to the essence or value of that image echoes one of Webster's definitions of *translation*: "being conveyed from one place to another; removed to heaven without dying." Her intense focus goes beyond mere self-expression rooted in the ego. These poems are self-explorations intensely wrought, bodied-forth, and magical, so that self-expression and revelation of the world are one and the same. As these poems vary in structure and kinds of revelation, they energize the understanding, signify the poet's dedication to change, to grow, to see things anew. Church's cumulative effect on the reader was what Thoreau, whose works she studied, advocated in his notebook, Thursday, Dec. 10, 1840:

> I discover a strange track in the snow, and learn that some
> migrating otter has made across from the river to the wood,
> by my yard and the smith's shop, in the silence of the
> night.—I cannot but smile at my own wealth when I am
> thus reminded that every chink and cranny of nature is full
> to overflowing—that each instant is crowded full of great
> events.

Such poetry that translates and relates, is likely organic and
revolutionary, so that in this collection of Church's poems we
discern not simply the static, realistic image, but the search for a
form to accommodate meaning and thus the connection the poet
makes in the act of writing between inner and outer worlds. In
writing "to keep from getting lost," the poet activates the paradox
common to all art. For Church, these images, these objects activate
the very self "lost" in the service of this dedication. As she
commented to Sarton in regard to her life, "solitude is a way of
waiting for the inaudible and the invisible to make itself felt."

Like most lyric poets, Church tends to want to write a longer
narrative and thus implies in the repeated motifs, themes, and images
the connections between poems. If, then, the poem serves as a study
in inner autobiography—symbolic event in the poet's life—then
taken together this collection constitutes a narrative, a story of that
life. Church saw connections between her writing and external
events. Often she would leap up during a conversation and read
a poem to make a point. She also held that plot or action was what
activated the primordial or archetypal image so that, taken to-
gether, these poems make a symbolic story. Like Jung, she believed
that art consists of the unconscious activation of an archetypal
image. The artist's unsatisfied yearnings reach back to a "voice" or
what Jung called the collective unconscious. The artist discerns the
psychic elements that play a part in the life of the collective.

Church, who said she was "up to her ears in mythology" (as
well as listening to the Rio de los Frijoles), richly taps both sources.
Denise Levertov, in describing this "rhythm of the inner voice of
the poet," explains this gift further:

What it means to me is that a poet, a verbal kind of person, is constantly talking to himself, inside of himself, constantly approximating and evaluating and trying to grasp his experience in words. And the 'sound' inside his head of that voice is not necessarily identical with his literal speaking voice, nor is his inner vocabulary identical with that which he uses in conversation. At their best sound and words are song, not speech. The written poem is then a record of that inner song.

Treating as she did the shifting issues which caused conflicts between the old and the new, Church reconciles, as Jung advocated, the insight of the artist and the needs of society, the pattern of her poems a bridge between both.

As Church once said about Haniel Long's poetry and life as a poet, the "finding" of one's life is a heady experience that one desperately wants to share. "It is as though one held in one's hand the mustard seed that might become the greatest of all trees and longs to summon all the birds of the air to shelter in it." In the quest for the enriched and shared life in the poem, the reader may feel as she did when describing the search for the seldom-given, almost perfect poem: "It is as though, walking among sand grains on an ancient riverbed, we come upon the perfectly formed crystal of which all others are only appromixations." With these poems, stones that they are—birds, bread, stones—we hold in one hand the warm remnant of a mountain. Haniel Long once wrote Church: "You know how for a poet everything is a symbol and we write only for those who will understand us." Church's gift is such that she makes poets of us all.

—*Shelley Armitage*
Lanikai, Hawaii

PART
ONE

*Love's
Genius*

After Looking into a Genealogy

Time is not, when I remember you, my grandmothers.
Your bones, your flesh have gone into the dust;
From granite stones the wind has wiped your names.
The years have trod your graves flat with the earth,
You who were beautiful, you who died still young
In childbirth, you who saw
Ninety and more full years before you passed,
Whose husbands died at sea, whose husbands died
In the stern winters of a wilderness.

Time is not, when I remember you, my grandmothers.
Mercy and Lydia and Abigail,
Ruth and Mehitable; sea-captains' wives,
Daughters of soldiers, mothers of men of God;
Statira, Betsey, Patience, Margery,
Remember, whose other name the gravestones have
        forgotten.

Out of old books these names, from moldering stones,
All that is left of you, my grandmothers!
        All but the blood
That makes me one with you. The blood that cried
Like a wanderer returned when I first saw—
I, the desert-born, this offspring
        of New England growing
Among New Mexico mountains—when I first saw
The dogwood blossoming in Connecticut woods,
The meadows sprinkled with a rain of daisies,
The apple-orchard set in low, green hills.

I know now why in my dreams I had seen those hills
      and had remembered
The covered bridges over Vermont rivers,
And why, whenever I came upon a clearing
      in mountain country
I thought: One could build a house here.
That slope would make a pasture. An orchard
      would be fruitful
In a few years, and the apples fragrant.
The butter I'd churn would be cool and sweetened
In a stone house over this mountain-spewed
      thread of water.

When I was a little girl
My mother kept the milk in a house
      built half underground
With shelves around the walls. There the warm milk
      yellowed
With heavy cream in rows of shallow pans. Something
      familiar,
Something not remembered first stirred in me
When I crept down to watch her.
But most of all, my grandmothers, your blood leaps
      in me
(Obliterating time, making of me one person with my
      forebears,
One person who has lived since life crawled up
      from the waters
And became man, who will not die
Till the last woman of this race is barren)
Most of all, my blood stirs with your voices
When the winds of winter thunder like ocean water
And the white snow whirls down in utter darkness.

Then I remember, or it seems as if I remembered,
The earliest winter, and the fierce grey water
Heaped between us and England (that grey water
Cradling more than one of my grandfathers)
The desperate stand we made against that winter,
The bitter battle.

We were sturdy-limbed, the daughters of that winter.
We had inherited strength that must be tried.
      We could not
Live and grow old, unrestless, in security,
And so we went off, shoulder to shoulder with our men,
      and singing,
Into the farther wilderness.

In these days, my grandmothers, the weak live easily.
The weak crowd out the strong like weeds
      in an untilled garden.
Where can we go, we in whom your blood sings?—
The eager blood of our forefathers, of our foremothers,
      who marched chin forward
And always toward the horizon?

Do Not Feel Sure

Do not feel sure that she will be long contented
In this house you have built for her.
She will love it all for a while. She will love to stir
Softly out in her kitchen all alone,
Placing her thin blue cups along the shelves
Spread with white paper;
Pinning a row of dripping towels, sky-blown
Like checkered sails to a frosty, silver wire;
Or cutting with one quick, eager turn of wrist
Into a bright gold orange.
You'll not believe that she can ever tire
Of resting tranquilly in your embrace,
Turning her sun-flushed face
Up to your cooler one to have it kissed,
Or seeking the warm, sure shelter of your hand
For her firm-fingered one.
But I know she was not meant for times like these.
She was made to dwell
Upon a stern dark edge of wilderness,
To watch men hew the barrier line of trees
And lay them log on log; with her own hands
To chink the wall that kept the wind outside.
She would have borne ten children sturdily,
Strong, brown-limbed boys and tall, wind-ripened girls.
Eager for bearing as a fertile tree,
She would not be appeased by mothering
One child or two as women are today.
She was not meant to buy life ready-made
But to do battle for it.
Someday she'll go
Swift as a loosened fox across the snow
And you'll not see her anymore.
How do I know?

6

Well, I've known wild things bred a hundred years
Till they forget the look of winter moons,
Silver of frost splintered on autumn grass,
The click of a pointed hoof, the cry of loons;
Till they forget the quiet, fear-white land,
The sharp-ribbed, silent hunger stalking it,
And what it is for parent beasts to stand
With strong, fierce pride between the seeking death
And their blind, whimpering young.
She is like that!
But the first, familiar shadow will waken her,
Or the first faint flicker of a star-sent cry
Or an old, old hunger making remembered stir
Will call her back more than a hundred years.
For all your tears
She will not once look back. If you are wise
You will not often let her be alone
To listen to the wind or watch the skies.
You will not let her bear one child for you
Lest in her ecstasy and in her pain
She should awaken to her hungry need
Of mothering ten.
When once she knows, she will not rest again
Or turn to you or pay you any heed.
She will make flight too swift for you to follow
Like a fear-fleet deer, or a wild, wind-driven swallow.

Shadow-Madness

They say her house is shadow-haunted now
Who while she lived loved shadows more than life.
She sought them everywhere. A saffron bough
Of autumn leaves was lovelier to her
If imaged upward from a pool of rain—
Reflections lie so softly with no stir
On wind-neglected water!

    In her room
She tempted shadows with smooth surfaces,
Loving the way the shapes of common things
Bent into strangeness. Even orchard bloom
Was only sweet when on her wall the moon
Painted the silver image.

    Every day
She polished carefully each knife and spoon
To see them shine; rubbed rainbows once again
Into each glass; then finished washing up
By blowing bubbles through her finger-tips.
The curving image of each star-gold cup
Hung soap-imprisoned for bewitching her.

She married one in whom she seemed to see
Her love reflected. She had thought to show
The magic of her shadow-world to him,
But he was bound fast to reality.
He liked a thing for its essential form,
Not the distorted image that it cast;
And so she slipped away from him at last.
He held her body but her thoughts became
Fleeting as images of blowing leaves

Wind-blurred on water. He was not to blame
Who could not grasp intangibility,
For she had been created shadow-mad
And vanished like the shadow with the flame.

Bridal

The slow wind rippled moonlight on the floor
While she lay wakeful. Rustling feet soft-furred
Spread rings of sound in the grass like water-blurred
Shadows of splashing leaves. Beyond the door
Fell a flood of silver light that seemed to pour
In showers from all the trees. Far off she heard
The questioning call of a star-awakened bird
And thought she could not lie there anymore
Against his arm. She would have slipped from bed
And run, moon-white, far up the fragrant lane
Of heavy-flowering trees. She would have stood
Star-cooled upon the hill above the wood.
But suddenly he stirred and woke again
And sleepily stretched his arm beneath her head.

Whom God Hath Joined

And does God join through word of man?
Were we made one by priestly word?
by anything we said that day?
by anything we heard?

Were we made one by act of flesh,
by ancient hungers stirred and fed?
Why then, the aching times we lay
lonely in marriage bed?

Why then, the struggle and the tears,
the two in conflict ceaselessly,
oneness so perilously born
out of the you and me?

Oh, stranger far than book and ring
the woven oneness two may know
who from self's ruined battleground
have watched their own hearts grow;

who see, with wonder on their lips,
with eyes tear-cleansed and opened wide,
that struggle, each for his own soul,
was struggle side by side!

1942

11

Prothalamium for Barbara

Will your marriage be as simple as Navaho?
Will you be to him earth and all curved surfaces?
Will he be to you lightning and the eagle's feather?
Will his gods be yours or will you both together
weave a new myth for your children?

Will your marriage be as complicated as Anglo-Saxon?
Your own people having no male, no female
deities—no metaphors of earth and heaven
to reconcile man with woman, winter with summer
midday with midnight, the morning star with the evening?

Or will your hands and his together hold the rainbow
the bridge between you, neither crossing over,
neither creating the other in his own image,
content to be to each other the bow and the bowstring
that speed to their unknown mark the future's arrows?

1946

Evergreen

Dear, I have watched the wind upon the hill
Running to take the birch trees with caress;
And I have watched the maple leaves athrill
Desirous of his touch. With blowing dress
White aspens run,—they really almost run,
Eager as girls to take their lover's kiss.
Sometimes I wonder, would you have me be
Birch-like, or maple-like, show eager bliss
Like aspens when they're kissed? Oh not for me
Their wild, ecstatic ways. I am a fir
Meeting the wind with vast tranquillity.
I seem to take your love with little stir;
But—autumn strips a birch tree of its song,
While firs are evergreen the whole year long!

Letter to Virginia

Do you remember those days, Virginia,
when we were young and Time was innocent?
The ripe world flowered around us.
Disaster was a seed whose spear had not thrust through
    the quiet earth.
We lay at night, embraced in peace by our husbands.
We gave birth to our children.
The days were luminous. The vines were sweet above
    the porches.
Thunder did not appall us; the mountains hung with
    rainbows.
At dusk we walked among moon-flowers. The children
    cried at bedtime.
After they slept we sang, we and the young men together
gathered around the piano in the firelight.

How young we were; how certain of the happy ending.
We planted trees and dreamed of the full harvest,
and dreamed of old age under the quiet branches.

But Time split like a dried seed.
The sleeping gods woke; the dead myths came alive;
lightning fell out of heaven and clashed among us.
We were uprooted from peace like trees in the
    great storm.
We found life is not what we dream, but something
    that dreams us.
Now if the dreamer tosses in nightmare what shall
    wake him?
Never again shall he dream those days of wonder.

But I shall remember you forever, Virginia,
the day that we stood together in the garden
and you knew that your love must die.
I shall remember how you stood in the wind like a
    flag unbeaten,
like the figurehead of a ship that faces the
    wave's crash,
proud and unvanquished, grown to the stature of woman.
The past fell behind you like a discarded plaything.
You gathered your children's hands and marched toward
    the future.

                                                    1944

On a Morning

On a morning
when the mountains were walls of fire
and the clouds like
curled smoke,
the blossoms of many trees were
flames of another color.
I stood with you
breast to breast,
pressed to you in an embrace without pressure,
your mouth upon my mouth,
out of us both, out of both our hearts a flame springing,
separately rooted,
arching over us,
merging into one flame
streaming upward,
absorbing quietly
the fire of the mountains,
mingling with itself
the burning blossoms.

And There Was Light

We have climbed this hill out of a black darkness,
a maelstrom of black darkness.

And now this,
this white night,
the snow sending the moon's light back again
shining and undisturbed,
and the dark sky, blue, oh deeply blue,
bluer than ever daylight was but dark,
and the stars shining.

Standing upon this hill
and joy like a light within me,
I and the stars singing the same song,
and this light including us all.

I will soar in a moment
upon the translucent snow,
fitting my skis to the curve of the hill,
soaring as the hill curves,
cleaving moonlight,
cleaving the still air,
tracing the pattern of flight upon the smooth snow,
over the arc of the white hill.
Making a pattern of beauty
in this winter night,
making a pattern
out of the joy in my heart,
out of my love for you.

East of the Sun and West of the Moon

In the deep of night I lighted my candle and saw you sleeping,
beautiful as a hero, as a young god, as my beloved,
frank in your maleness, acquiescent to your beauty,
lying there lightly in pale light as a child lies.

I bent over you marvelling,
I bent over you in exaltation and in sorrow
knowing this for the moment out of fairy-tale
when the maiden first sees her love in his true shape, sleeping
and spills the tallow of her candle on his shoulder
so that he wakes and vanishes, and she must seek him
through the inevitable seven years of legend.

She must wander, questioning, through the wide world,
must cross the burning ploughshares, the fierce glass mountain,
and wake him from his sleep, and make him know her
forever as his true love.

In the deep of night I leaned over you, holding my candle
in terror and awe of this quest, this quest that must lead me
east of the sun and west of the moon until I find you
beautiful as a hero, as a young god, as my beloved
standing before me forever in your true shape.

Poem to Accompany the Gift of a Loaf of Bread

I give you the ploughed field,
the smell of the moist earth,
the first shine of rainfall,
the full seed burst open;
the fragily groping
pale-fingered blind roots;
the green spear of living
thrust splendidly upward.
I give you the sun for a
summer's full season,
the cold shine of moonlight;
the wind tossing green waves;
the stir of the little mice
under this canopy
under these grasses.

I give you all men who have
shaped the furrow:
the sower, the reaper;
the factory worker
who founded the metal,
who fashioned the stern plough;
he who guided the thrasher.
I give you their toil and their
sweat and their heartbreak,
their despair and their courage,
their strength and their tenderness.
I give you the mill and the
song of the millers,
older than Egypt,
as ancient as hunger.

I give you the harvest,
the hum of the reapers,
the noise of the thrashers;
the warm grain poured out in a
great golden river;
give you the fine flour
moistened and sweetened;
salted and leavened;
stirred with humility,
kneaded with reverence;
give you the risen dough
warm to the shaping touch,
live as a beating heart
under these urgent and
listening fingers.

I give you the bread at last
fragrant as springtime;
fashioned of earth and sun;
sweet as a summer field,
good as the gentle rain,
golden as harvest.
TAKE AND EAT, saith the Lord,
THIS IS THE SACRIFICE.
THIS IS MY BODY BOTH
BROKEN AND OFFERED.
THIS IS THE MYSTERY.
THIS IS THE LIVING GOD.
FEED ON HIM IN THY HEART
BY FAITH WITH THANKSGIVING.

The Woman Who Dwells

The woman who dwells at the place of healing by
    the river
sits singing and sings the shape of the gods from
    the four directions;
sings onto the horizon the four mountains where the
    gods dwell;
sings into the bare sky the small cloud moving in
    brightness;
sings into the bare earth the growing tip of the
    green corn;
sings the river into a singing curve around her;
sings herself into the center of herself, alive
    and listening.
The woman who dwells at the place of healing by the
    river
stirs not from her place, goes not to the far
    mountains,
soars not into the high sky, enters not the deep
    earth;
sings as she draws in the sand the circle of healing;
sings the gods from the four directions into that
    circle;
sings the growing cloud into the reach of her own
    heart;
sings herself into the spear of the green corn growing.

1939

Tilano of San Ildefonso
for Laura Gilpin

How many years, Tilano,
since you have been gone from us—
yet you live still in this portrait,
the lines of your face like the lines on a contour map,
the mountains become rivers,
the wind's gesture.

Behind you a cornfield,
the stalks standing tall.
The long leaves seem to rustle
in air made visible through the camera's magic.
The leaves have the shape of wings,
long-winged birds,
the sandhill crane, the heron,
about to rise in flight.

There is a cloud behind you
in which the corn is mirrored.
The narrow stalks have the shape of holy beings
drawn on a sacred stone.
Pollen is shaken
in a day-long dance
downward on leaves and tassels.
The corn is maiden
and man in one,
fruit, and the fructifier.

The camera's eye
teaches our own to see beyond surfaces.
The corn is an image of your inner being
and you its human partner.
You have come a long way together
under the wrenching winds,

22

under the bare sun.
There is something triumphant in your gaze;
you have known what it is to sustain life.

Your face, Tilano,
has man and woman in it,
sternness and tenderness,
darkness and molding light.
You smile,
yet your lips are not parted;
your eyes speak their own language.
We must read your face like a leaf
or a finger-print,
the trace of a shell,
the incised music of
a vanished ocean.

1971

Peñas Negras

We walked in the early morning to the graveyard,
setting out before the sun had risen,
the flowers heavy in our arms, and the green blanket woven
by your loving hands to cover the grave of your mother.
This day, Corina, I came to know tenderness
that had long been buried in the graveyard of my own heart.

This morning I put aside my proud thought and walked beside you
to Peñas Negras, the valley of the black rocks,
and walked beside you, like a child, with my arms full of iris.
The meadowlarks sang, and the dew lay like a mystery on the tall grass.
The mountains were jewels of light on the cold horizon.
You knelt and plucked the wild grass from the grave and spread over it
        the blanket you had woven.
You set flowers at the head and the feet;
roses of paper among the petals of roses
bloomed upon the fallen crosses in the graveyard.

Oh I might have smiled at you once for this unreasoning gesture
of love toward the unliving. Yet a spirit was incarnate
in your face and your pose as you knelt there, a wisdom of woman
that had been born of loving. I saw how the maternal
is more than the flesh and the bones of the mortal mother.
Through my sudden tears I saw how your mother had taught you
from her place in your heart all that your child's heart needed
to make it a woman's. Then I too knelt
and placed my flowers beside yours, and received this blessing.

1948

24

Elegy in Three Movements for Alice and Haniel Long

1.

As they grew older—
he already half blind, she indomitably more frail
as though for his sake she allowed time to gnaw her only in secret—
we, knowing how she had been the tree
on which the vine of his life twined,
yes, twined and flowered with all its weaving tendrils
reaching with sensitive tips toward sunlight and moonlight,
had dreaded the inevitable death that must come to one of them
first in the fading of the long day's journey.
The leaves of their lives were so inextricably mingled
it seemed as though their roots must have become one root.

This was more true than we dreamed.
When the surgeon's last skill failed him
it was she who died first, as though they'd a common heart.
Though he was far from home, mysteriously knowing
that all was not well, she hurried ahead of him,
with a last effort of her exhausted will
upsetting even death's protocol
to make, if she could, the last darkness seem familiar
like a mother who lights her child to bed with a steady candle.

It was as though she being gone,
he still unknowing yet, began to bleed
his own sap back into the deep mulched earth
in which their roots were hid.
How shall we say it was not a happy ending
for two whose lives were joined into one music?
The last chords sound; the musician's hands fall slowly,
and every discord now resolves in silence.

2. The Unicorn

I think he kept a unicorn
in his garden, or even himself was
partly a unicorn and reverted to the form at certain
seasons, or under the influence of the moon or
the scent of unidentified herbs,
or the echo of hoofbeats among the constellations
inaudible to most ears.

It was a difficult affliction
to bear with, the unicorn being
something unclassifiable, mythological,
not zoological in an age when
almost no one believes in mythology.
If Leda were to confess the swan rape or
Danae blame her condition on a
god in a ray of gold, you know what they'd be called now!
So he was always careful to
hide the flaw in his heredity from the literal minded
who were often a bit puzzled
by the sharp rim of a hoofprint among the roses in the garden
or a tree rubbed by an aching horn.

As it turned out
he was in his most serious danger from maidens
who fancied they saw in him a resemblance
to something they had once dreamed of.
Their eager looks often threatened
to give him away, for he could never entirely
escape the unicorn's need of cooling its chafed horn
between their indulgent breasts.
There were few of them who understood they were dealing
with a legendary creature
who in his human form was undoubtedly
the most faithful and uxorious of husbands.

Married to a fat and
placid wife entirely preoccupied
as far as anyone could see with her sewing and ironing,
with a baby voice and almost no charm of conversation,
nevertheless it was to her he returned unfailingly
like the unicorn in the legend to the lap of the virgin.

Was she the antithesis of everything wild, I wonder?
Was it really she who kept him human?
Some thought it a pity but
what if the unicorn strain had won out?
Together they tamed it to live quite peacefully in the garden
among the cabbages and the roses.
Sometimes at teatime
I've thought I saw it curled between them like a good dog
whose quicksilver eyes laughed at us a little from a far world.

3. Love Was Their Genius

My wife maintained an air of calm and love.
—Haniel Long

Love was their genius,
love presiding among us at the tea hour,
kindled over and over on the warm hearth,
reflected from their faces in the firelight.

Love was the air she maintained,
her content with being woman
and with his being man, his helplessness,
his strength where she had none.

Love was the old-fashioned motto she embroidered
for him like a child in cross-stitch;
it was the valentine he gave her,
his beating heart pierced by the silver arrow.

Love was the deaths he died
to all that was not love, over and over
yielding his vulnerable
flesh and his blood to the burning and the terror,

and coming back to find her steady presence
like daybreak in a dark room.
Love was the mirror
she kept unclouded for him.

Love was the lesson that they learned together
from flowers and earth and sun;
it was the cryptogram whose secret meaning
they read lifelong between them.

Love was the token they gave us,
the leaf on the path, the sentence underlined,
the flower pressed and hidden between the pages,
the curved shell left on the shore

for our hands to hold after the green wave slowly
dies back into the sea.

1956

Alas

Alas, my love I grow older.
The nights seem colder.
Morning no longer
sings me awake as it used to
with birds
or the sound of fish leaping.
The nets that I cast for my dreams
are torn and too heavy
to lift out of the draining water.

Day breaks
and I lie in my bed
like a chick
feeling my warmth curved
close as a shell around me.
There is frost on the window.
Ice crystals live and
growing into forests.
The sun will rise soon and melt them.
The slow fires that burn in my blood
even while I sleep, and keep it moving,
do not warm me as well as they used to.
The stars seem colder.

I do not dream of love anymore,
only sometimes of death in deep waters.
What will it seem like, I wonder, not to waken?
The world will go on, I know—
summer and winter,
morning and evening,
birds coming back in spring,
the rivers carving valleys
and filling them up again,

seas rising and falling.
But what when the eye does not wake
to see or the heart to sing it?

How I begrudge the body's slow death;
would rather be seized and eaten
by an eagle or a sharp fish
than by this inward worming.
Must we live at the last in a house with dirty windows
and doors that will not open,
the chimneys clogged and the hearthfire grown too sluggish
to make real flames anymore?
To desire nothing anymore
except sleep?
If one could only
spin some kind of a cocoon
and then wait mindless
as a caterpillar that winters on a bare branch.

1963

Elements for an Autobiography

1.

The gold cowslip
alluring far off
at the center of the black muck
she dared not wade through
to touch.

2.

Coughing at night
in the dark house
with the curved bannister.
The old patriarch
lies asleep.
They come at night warning her
not to,
not to wake grandfather.
If she does not
they will give her, they say,
a shiny pin of silver
shaped like a little boat.

3.

Mushrooms in the damp woods,
lichens spreading
over granite their
rosy or leaf-colored
longing for symmetry.

4.
Horses:
the sweet smell of leather, the
cold bit
stained green,
the long reins dragging
behind her
as she slyly creeps up
to the wild hoofed one in the pasture.

1971

Lament

Ancient camels
crossing a puddle of hot rock
left indelible footprints.
Your footprints still startle me
into aching recollection.

The tools left hanging in your workshop:
the little knife you gave me
like the one you always carried
wherever you were,
in the car, on picnics,
to open whatever needed to be opened,
to dig out splinters,
to tighten loose screws
when the world seemed to be falling apart.

It is the workman in you that I weep for:
the squares and levels,
saws all shapes and sizes,
nails for every imaginable place or purpose,
screwdrivers, nuts and bolts—
there was nothing you would not try
to make or mend.

You are gone now.
How often my own life seems past any mending.

1975

Shattered

A dog barked
and shattered the chrysalis of silence.
I came out of my dream
and found the stars had moved
only a handsbreadth down the indefinite arc
of heaven.
You and I were two people again
contained in two bodies,
and the long wave shattered beneath our hands
and went out
on the sands of morning.

1934

Cat and Cosmos

In the early morning before rising I read "The History
    of Nature."
My young cat beside me gazes wondering.
To her, perhaps, I am myself a cosmos
beyond the reach of sense. She can see only
the surfaces of being.
Her eyes flicker at the sound of this pencil on the paper.
Her pupils widen. She follows the track of the pencil on the
    white page,
knowing nothing of words that form here.
I gaze at the pictures of nebulae, the curve of light-forms
    on far space.
The cat comes closer,
stares into my eyes with love pinpointed in her green gaze.
The nebulae swirl through my thought,
clouds, rotating forms, spheres, vanishing vapors,
the explosions and pressures of space, light concentrated upon
    prisms,
the astronomer's dreaming eye.
The cat's eyes widen like curtains exposing black moons.
The iris is green and gold, shaded like petals.
She curls closer to share my warmth.
My cat is energy wrapped in skin and warm fur,
sun's heat compressed in this strict yet fluid outline.
Light decorates her in mute patterns. Her ears are mobile
antennae that focus sound.
She and I speak without words. We do not confuse each other
with subtleties of language. She interprets voices
as I do music. When our eyes meet
the currents of our lives join.
Swifter than light through space. We have both travelled
enormous distance since our world broke from the sun's heart.
I think there is even a little of the reptile

within us still, as well as of light's pure essence.
But she in her flesh-locked form is innocent of all fate.
Her eyes, piercing mine, cannot trace the light that shines there
to its origin in the cosmos, nor perceive time's arrow
fallen to final rest.
Beyond my vision,
as mine beyond hers, is the thought behind the arrow
whose language I do not know, the image hidden
in the life that throbs at my wrist, the light that forms
        words
into shapes of suns and of moons on my inward darkness.

                                                        1954

Portrait of My Father

Great child, blue-eyed,
beseeching always, "Love me."
Bull in a china shop on purpose;
everything we cherished
you mocked and then plead, "Love me."
How could we help loving
you for the wistful child who
gorged himself on strawberries,
then (guilty) spanked *us*?
Incorrigible,
yet we must *never* be.
Loving,
yet fearing nothing so much as love,
you raged like a volcano
through our placid domestic days.
Sitting up all night with a sick dog,
next day you would kick it downstairs
for failing to obey you.
I have seen you lash a
stubborn horse till its sides wept,
yet no one could be more gentle.
It was you who
bandaged our hurt knees, brought us water at night when
we were fevered.
You said when you were dying
"I would crawl on my hands and knees to help anyone sick,"
and you would have.

Great clown, your foolery
was the cap and bells of our childhood,
yet my heart still is
full of unhealed wounds where a barbed word
found too easy a mark and festered.

Hero and warrior, you
were rider of stallions,
rescuer from floods,
fire fighter and
first nurse of my infancy.
Womb-rejected into December cold
you wrapped me like your lamb in wool,
through many fierce nights fostered
the premature flame of my life.
I rode wild horses to please you,
walked narrow logs over torrents
but you never noticed.
You became the ring master
cracking his long whip snakelike
at my failures.
So I married to escape you,
bore dutiful sons and
let none of them grow in your image.
Oh how can I now untie this
cord of umbilical love that binds me to you
as though I were your grave?

1956

The Return

After the days through which we drove imprisoned
by tongues of landscape barren of translation,
we came to this room that was curtained in pinafores;
the prayerbook breathed on the square of the marble table;
grandfather bureaus bent their brows around us;
night ringed us with owls and with sheep-bells.
We slept in a husk of ourselves, in a rustle of dry years;
the wallpaper sang to us with child eyes like a garland.

Brought to this bed between the wordless candles,
godfather borne to the place of our unnaming,
we lay habited in sleep like holy orders,
beyond sex or penetration held each other
in a slow September music of returning
to the forgiven tree.

The journey and the years fell backward from us;
the swords couched sleeping in the eyes of angels;
in the bare crotch of night the bird was songless,
warm and unfledged. I laid my hand upon you
as though you were my child and felt the swarming
of stars and instruments.

When morning broke me
out of your side, we groped through aisles of mirrors
receding into dream.

1957

The Agéd Man
for John Gaw Meem

The agéd man sang in my dream.
I heard him sing
love of his long years,
love of the bright flame
that blazed up and consumed
his life's last remnant.
I heard the gathered song
pour from his wasted frame
and fill the room
and echo in the caverns of my heart.
Music became a fire
that fed itself on every mortal part
like flame on knotted wood.
How could an agéd man find strength to sing
approaching his life's end?
In dream I went to him and knelt
and laid my face between his knees and wept
while that music rose within me like a sea.

Silly Song for My Eightieth Birthday
for Nancy Wirth

She said, "You are not going to be an octogenarian.
What you will become this year is an octogeranium."
Ten times eight is an octogeranium.
A geranium is a cranesbill.
A cranesbill is a wildflower.
Hermes invented the alphabet when he saw cranes flying.
    The book says
"Standing in water the crane is the first to welcome
Dawn when she rises,"
when, I suppose, the ripples reflect scarlet.
The scarlet geranium is the birthday flower of my birthday.
On December the first I am going to become a scarlet geranium,
or a flock of cranes flying in alphabetical angles,
or one crane alone waiting for the splash of daybreak.
All this because of a simple mistake in spelling,
enough to make Hermes laugh who invented letters to spell with.
It is he I invoke with his wand to complete my transformation,
or at least to make it happen in my mind's eye.

1983

41

On Reading Pablo Neruda

My hair bristles on the back of my neck
sometimes when I read Pablo Neruda,
as though his life were becoming my life,
his childhood
echoing my own,
the other half of a hemisphere,
a soul singing
in counterpoint
with mine.
How can this be?
How is it possible to enter into
the life of another being?
The poet in me
responds to this other life,
to the life that flowers within us,
the origin of words,
as though at the source,
at the headwaters,
the hidden fountain of all singing
we both are one.
My own childhood
emerges beside his
or his
joins mine,
two tributaries
that meet and flow toward a common ocean.

1982

The Sonnets (Selected)

I.

Some I have seen whom the years case in stone.
The vein's quicksilver chills. The docile mind
settles into firm grooves. Inflexible bone
determines motion. Heart becomes wish confined
in rigid crystal worn for ornament.
They who once dreamed themselves Tristan-Isolde
walk now invulnerable to dream, their sorrow spent,
their joy a fallen star enshrined and cold.
But you and I, my dear, began with stone
armored upon our hearts defiantly.
The winds and weathers of our years have blown
all our defences down and set us free.
Let us walk forth now on our ripened fields
and pluck what fruits of love the season yields.

IV.

I have been more alone sometimes than I can say.
We have lived so close, and yet so far apart.
You have armored yourself in routine of every day.
You have hidden your thought from me and all
    your heart.
Now round and round the close-chinked wall I go
and weep and tear my hands, yet cannot find
among the quarried stones piled row on row
the smallest entrance to your heart upon the air,
only the echo of my voice returns
waking no harmony against the bare
and adamant bastions. No tender ferns,
no delicate ivy clings upon that wall.
No secret door swings open at my call.

V.

Yet I must love the crystal of your soul
although no metamorphosis of rain
or tears can penetrate its whole
and geometric pattern. Rooted grain
can never feed upon that element
so firmly fixed in pure polarity.
Even the waves of light are only bent
and untransformed by living alchemy.
So strangely married, you that cannot yield
being fixed within your essence; I that cry
against your rock's hard core, the infertile field
that nourishes no root. Yet till I die
who could not flower upon this impervious stone
I am shaped upon your shape like flesh on bone.

VIII.

Once I was seed within my mother's womb
and was at peace, unwakened, unaware
until life's seminal arrow cleft that tomb
and split me from myself. So now I bear
the difficult pattern of duality
within my blood, my bone, and cry and strive
against the mute, the stern polarity
that while it rends, yet makes all life alive.
So I have struggled with you endlessly
in outward semblance of the inner war
between the yes and no, the he, the she,
in my own elements. My secret core
opposes yours, and yet within your soul
I seek my severed self to be made whole.

X.

What ill enchantment blinded my two eyes
that I could never love you? I was cursed
by what malevolent fairy? What disguise
admitted her to work her evil worst
upon my christening, pronounce me blind,
or, fate more grievous than Titania bore,
decree that in my husband's face I find
only the ass's head that Bottom wore?
What evil dream bore I within my breast
that would not let me love? For now I know
love is the greater magic that confessed
in all its name's full power must overthrow
dreams, visions, bad enchantments. With sure hand
I draw its circle round us in the sand.

XII.

To love: to be possessed, or to possess?
To give oneself? To strive to make one's own?
What errors of blind thought we must confess
who from our childhood's wilfulness have grown
to know that love and will are opposite
as light and weight are. Love may not be spoken
in the same breath that says, "I want," nor woken
where one says, "I submit."
Like earth and moon our wills have always striven
to hold or to escape. Now in our heaven
of complementary life we have been woven
into a destiny of tides, of balanced motion.
Will holds us centered in this whirling flight;
Love is reflection, each to each, of light.

XIII.

To love. To know. Are these two then the same?
The effort of the heart, the mind, the will
seeking to penetrate, not to consume. To name.
To recognize. To touch. To fill
oneself with knowing as the sea with light
beneath the break of day. To know. To love.
To take into the heart the dark, the bright.
To drink the contents and yet be the cup.
To love as we should love a star, a stone,
not for our greed of light nor hope for bread
but for the star's blind need of eyes, the tone
of words within the rock none yet has said.
Thus do we love at last whose ripened choice
is to be toward all things the eyes, the voice.

XIV.

Love is not gazing in another's eyes,
finding another fair, nor being found,
not tenderness to hush another's cries,
nor strength that lifts one, fallen, from the ground.
Love is two faces set toward one star
that two who see may mark as their own north,
and set their course by it however far
their separate paths may wander back and forth.
Love is a fabric on which two threads weave
the Bird of Paradise, the Tree of Life,
the ancient disobedience of Eve,
the serpent twined between the Man, the Wife.
It is the tree that marries earth to sky
created of her dust, his blazing eye.

XV.

For F.S.C. 1900-1975

I am thinking this morning of the beauty of the earth
as you and I both loved it, wondering
how my vision is still half yours—the broken surf
of morning over landforms; slant light; rolling thunder
at the edge of our summer picnics; the high dancing
flight of the sandhill cranes, their cry that echoed
like water rippling over smooth stones, over the far
       expanse of
bright air. Within and all around us time flowed,
making, unmaking mountains: the crystal essence
still glitters in the sand grains of dry rivers.
Nothing seems lost—light's changes, wind-swept silence,
the arid land reflecting the shape of water.
I gather pebbles feeling your quiet presence
companion me still in all we loved together.

PART
TWO

*The Rose,
Unfurling*

School Boy

You sat at table with me yesterday
who had not met with hunger all your life,
not in your own bone nor another's face
pressed close to yours, or smiting like a knife
at your impervious heart. You broke your bread
with young, unthinking greed, and took your fill
of all your father's wealth had bought for you,
acknowledging no debt, no gratitude
for the great blessing of our common food.

Yet since I thought you had a human heart,
and since the human heart shares joy and grief
and knows its oneness thus, I shared with you
a tale of human woe beyond belief
that happened in our day: how Christian men
had turned a ship of exiled souls away
from shore on shore through winter month on month
until at last the weaponed enemy
turned friend and sank them in the forgiving sea.

You looked across your plate at me and laughed:
"That surely was a joke on them," you said,
"The funniest thing I've ever heard," you said,
and spread some more jam on your piece of bread.
Oh I was angry at you then, but angrier
at us, your teachers, fathers, mothers, all
who'd never taught your heart to feel for man;
who'd stuffed your mind but kept your heart asleep;
who'd let you think that men must never weep.

We fed you the bleached bones of history,
all the technique of grammar, ancient war
declined and conjugated expertly.
We did not teach you what your soul is for.
We send you forth upon the innocent land
armed with such power as heaven has never dreamed.
You do not know man's soul must act for God.
Who can we find to take compassion's part
when we have taught no mercy to the heart?

Omens

I have seen omens in the sky,
and in the entrails of wild beasts slaughtered;
have felt the ground pulse without footfall;
watched dead leaves driven by no wind.

I know too how blood runs from the slit vein,
the bitter taste of blood on the lips,
the slow cup filling,
the sacrificial gesture;

have seen the hero strip himself of his armor
and come before me in the dark tent;
Oh beautiful body, naked and vulnerable;
I have held him defenceless through the long night

and have not shuddered when I saw him carried
under the knees and arms between two soldiers,
his lips clenched upon death, his head hung backward,
both eyes awake and staring at the dead sky.

On a heap of broken walls I have found the point of an
        arrow,
cold stone, vindictive, all that was left of hatred,
and a pot broken, all that was left of hunger.

Sic Transit Gloria

We have gazed too often on the ruined cities.
Since childhood they were our playground. We were
    reminded
daily that men must die. Their bones were hidden
in the anonymous earth. Their cities, fallen,
were grass-swept mounds. The altars where they worshipped
lay open to the sky. We did not know the
name of the god they had chosen to protect them.
Pityingly at times we imagined the women who had walked
    there
bearing the water jars from the steep canyon
in the beauty of morning and evening. We imagined the
    hunters
piercing the forest shadows with alert eye.
The cities were fortresses, but they had fallen
besieged by what enemy we knew not, or overtaken
by what shifts in time's strange and enormous weathers.

We were the living. We were the twigs unfolding
at the tip of a great tree. The sap surged through us
in an unbroken column. Our roots dug deep
among the crumbled rocks of a time past
from which we still were nourished. Our history united
us with another continent. The blood of England
was channeled in our veins still; Saxon and Norman
bequeathed us their heroes. Even the Mediterranean
waters sang in our dreams. The Adriatic
and the Aegean seas were more familiar
in our tradition than the Atlantic harbors.
The garden of Eden had mothered our lost beginnings.
Who knows but that Abraham fathered us, and that we too
    marched
through the Arabic wilderness with Moses out of Egypt?

Thus for our roots. But now our branches are shaken
by equinoctial and autumnal weathers.
We who once laughed among the ruined cities
behold our own time go down in a ruin of dead leaves.
We weep for the splendor that we cherished, fallen
at our own hands. We weep that Time has chosen
us for the agents of our own destruction.
We have grown too wise. We have seen that life requires
        death.
We know that rocks must decay to feed roots, that the sun's
        destruction
is all that sustains us, that Time devours his children
yet himself engenders the hero that shall vanquish
the past, and inseminate the future. We read the seasons
with accurate premonition, knowing that when the fig tree
puts forth her leaf and bud, autumn must follow
as the night follows day, and we must perish.

We have worshipped too long the productions of our own
        hands
the images of god we have invented
to protect us from the God who has created
us in his terrible and uncompleted image. Our cathedrals
have been fortresses too long. Now life assails them,
guiding the lightning in our hands against our own wills.
We stand appalled upon the smoking ruins. Yes, the harvest
fields must be dunged with death. The hound of heaven
pursues us still, and all that we have hidden
shall be reclaimed. The harvest shall be winnowed
and all the chaff consumed. Our children's children
shall stand in wonder on the flowering ruins.

The Nuclear Physicists

These are the men who
working secretly at night and against great odds
and in what peril they knew not of their own souls
invoked for man's sake the most ancient archetype of evil
and bade this go forth and save us at Hiroshima
and again at Nagasaki.

We had thought the magicians were all dead, but this was the
     blackest of magic.
There was even the accompaniment of fire and brimstone,
the shape of evil, towering leagues high into heaven
in terrible, malevolent beauty, and, beneath, the bare trees
made utterly leafless in one instant, and the streets where no
     one
moved, and some walls still standing
eyeless, and as silent as before Time.

These are the men
who now with aching voices
and with eyes that have seen too far into the world's fate,
tell us what they have done and what we must do.
In words that conceal apocalypse they warn us
what compact with evil was signed in the name of all the
     living,
and how, if we demand that Evil keep his bargain,
we must keep ours, and yield our living spirits
into the irrevocable service of destruction.

Now we, in our wilderness, must reject the last temptation:
the kingdoms of earth and all the power and the glory,
and bow before the Lord our God, and serve Him
whose still small voice, after the wind, the earthquake,
the vision of fire, still speaks to those who listen
and will the world's good.

Master Race

The mountain, ancient and wise as myth,
created prophecies above our city
enormous and unheeded. Daily we witnessed
heroic marriages of light and darkness,
the births of heroes, the revolt of angels,
deities crowned and murdered, holy incests.
We were too proud to read unwritten wisdom.
We forbade any but our own tongue to be spoken.
Our knowledge had pierced all shrines and left them broken.

The former inhabitants whom we had made our servants
worshipped these wonders. They spoke with delicate gestures
of a god in the cloud, in the rainfall.
They honored the earth as woman;
in winter would not permit a wheel to turn upon her.
They prayed with eagle's feathers, with the hand shaking yellow pollen,
with the sound of the drum hid deep in the earth like a heartbeat.
There were times when this stirred in us something long forgotten,
or a thing not dreamed yet.

We knew what we knew:
that the earth was nothing sacred;
that the voice of our brother's blood would not cry against us;
that whatever we wanted from women could be taken.
There was nothing joined that we dared not put asunder.
We did not fall on our knees when we rent the atom.
We could look upon God and live. There was no wonder
our wisdom could not pierce in earth or heaven,
and claim for our possession.

When did the mountain cease to be our landmark?
When did we notice that our sky was barren?
When did a wilderness replace our marked roads?
We walked and seemed to stumble among ruins.
Stones, fallen, cried out in unfamiliar patterns.
Seeking, we could not find, hearing, all song was broken.
Our eyes did not weep for terror or for kindness.
We did not know at last whose children lead us,
nor if for scorn or pity of our blindness.

1948

Within

Within
fauns, satyrs, serpents,
the ruined fragments of
dead gods.
Only the serpent lives
whose eyes are topaz,
dormant and dreaming of
the resurrection.
I dreamed I was Bluebeard's wife.
I opened the closet.
There I beheld the mutilated corpses.
I touched the blood with my finger.
I fled forth screaming
to be hunted forever by the voice that cried
Thou shalt not.
I dreamed I was Eve in the garden,
the innocent,
the virtuous maiden with her hair in long braids.
I trusted in God the Father who said Thou shalt not.
The fruit of the tree in the garden was still
        unripened.
Then the serpent came winding up like a flame out
        of darkness.
I did not fear him; I did not know what fear was.
I ate of the golden apple that he gave me.
I ate and I did not die,
yet I fled screaming
from the angered voice of Thou shalt not
in the garden.

1944

59

San Felipe

They had been dancing all day
crowned with sky color, holding in their hands green
    branches.
All day they had been merged with one another,
and with the earth, the heaven.
After the dance was over
a few of them came to throw their boughs upon the water,
and we to whom prayer has become a spectacle
lined up at the river's edge to watch them.

It will be a shame, we said, when the Indians dance
    no longer;
and we spread our picnic things out in their holy places
and we stared at the men who stood praying beyond us
    without shame
in the ancient and beautiful gesture of the human heart
    humbled
we dared not dream what deities moved among us
nor dared to say what emptiness swept through us.

1948

Lost World

I dreamed we went, as once we used to go,
horseback across the mountain-high plateau
where once the wind was a transparent sea,
breaking in brightness over every tree,
pouring its light upon the golden grass
where we as children saw the wild deer pass,
and heard the turkey call, and the soft dove
intone her gentle memory of love.

Once more in dream our eager horses strode
the homeward-winding, summer-dusty road,
the saddle leather warm beneath our knees,
the steaming sweat, the aromatic trees,
the sharp, quick ring of hooves, the shaken manes,
the supple tension of the bridle reins,
Oh hand and mind and heart in unison,
the horse's wisdom and the man's made one!

Now all save this was changed. The road we knew
came to a gate and no one could pass through
who did not swear to look nor left nor right
and to forget whatever threatening sight
might meet his wayward glance. Stricken we stayed
until our claims to enter could be weighed
by guard whose face was frozen in a frown.
We looked within and saw the trees cut down,

and saw a city stand, and saw men there
given what they might ask to make life fair,
houses they had not built, and water towers,
effortless playthings for their leisure hours,
streets where the smallest child might safely run,
churches with tall spires gleaming in the sun,

yet every face there wore it seemed to me,
the look of creatures in captivity.

No man sang his own song. No children cried,
"Run, Sheep! Oh run, Sheep, run!" at eventide.
The soda fountain flowed; the juke box played.
Dogs tethered still felt wildness, sometimes bayed
the invisible moon; hardly a man at night
looked up to seek the stars' remembered light.
None called his house his own when day was done,
and no man loved the task he labored on.

Nor looked with joy upon his own child's face
so innocent of harm still in that place
where each man wove, in barred and secret room
some small fierce portion of his neighbor's doom.
Our patient horses stood with dragging rein
but time would not turn back for us again,
nor take the stain of terror from those skies
nor give us back our dream of Paradise.

1950

Andromeda's Question

Among the rocks the serpent crept
and stayed and coiled her venomous length
and rasped her warning on the air.
I bade you slay her for me there.
The snake, I said, was enemy
of all things innocent and good.
She came behind me where I stood,
a lightninged shadow, poised and swift
as death itself, as all that hates.
And I, like one who abdicates
a sovereignty, gave you the spear,
my own sharp steel, and womanwise
half-watched, half-turned away my eyes
from the stern sight of bloody death.
You struck, and struck remorselessly
and did what must be done, while I
rent by compassion, yet stood by
and felt the pain of each fierce blow
until the mangled, evil head
lay still upon the rocks, and dead.

I leaned and touched the lifeless thing.
I felt it harmless in my hands
that long had been my enemy,
my own blind animosity
that bade me hate where I would love,
be cruel where I would be kind,
the sharp, resistant, female mind
that shares no wisdom with the heart,
that guards itself and dwells apart,
and having driven love away,
lives solitary, blind with hate,
barring an empty Eden's gate.

To her all things that live and move
seem hostile, whether foul or fair
and she forever cries, Beware!
who loving not goes all unloved.
No gentle child may stretch his hand,
no bird whose heart is bright with song
but finds her poised, malign and strong.

We wait among the silent rocks.
Are you my angel half whose spear
unfliching drives toward its mark,
whose thought discerns the light, the dark,
the limits of the limitless,
whom neither gentleness nor tears
unmans when woman's face appears
among the Gorgon's writhing locks?
Are you the hand of God that wields
the thunderbolt till all his fields
are dunged with living blood? Alas,
can life be saved by nought but death?
Was this poor serpent's poisonous breath
more evil than the brandished spear
in your relentless human hand?
Should I have cried you to withhold
and knelt to cherish the unsouled
and frantic creature? Would my love
have armored me against her dart
and kindled in her breast a heart?

The night bends down above us now;
the evil thing lies still and cold.
No pity stirs the silent land.
And shall I turn and take your hand
that freed me from this serpent shape,
that lent itself to my black need?
Shall I now weep upon this deed

who cried to you that it be done?
Can God's great tenderness not bear
the deeds his own just hand must dare,
and are we not God's hand and heart?
Shall there be strife between us two?
I stand here now beside the slain,
not in wild triumph but in prayer.
Around me moves the formless air,
and death, I know, is not the end
for what is slain is but set free
to take another shape and live.
Was this, I ask, with strange surmise,
murder, or was it sacrifice?

1950

Driven

I drove with two strangers
through the dead world.
They did not know it was dead
or that we were already ourselves
ghosts.

The day of the buffalo had passed;
the day of the wagon train
and the Indians.
Cattle like playthings
dotted the dead landscape,
a mirage from
a time all three of us
vaguely thought we remembered,
already extinct as
perhaps we ourselves were.

The wide road with its dazzle
led on and on to hell
never arriving because
always already there.
"The Way *is* the goal"
someone told me once.
Neither of my companions
would have understood that.

One slept.
One turned up the radio.
Flotsam and jetsam
wallowed against our ears
cast up by stagnant oceans
in which the water of life had
long since been blotted and poisoned.

I kept looking up at the stars
like a drowning person
gulping fragments of air
before going down for the last time.
But the stars said no hope or promise;
their light spoke nothing to my dead ear,
having abruptly turned their backs on mankind,
my kind,

Lords of creation in the dead myth.

1966

Words for a Spring Operetta
in Walgreen's Payless Drugstore

Checking out
my package of Kaopectate,
the first in line at the check stand on a Saturday morning
in March,

I said to the girl with cinder smudges around her eyes
who kept the place of toll,
"But where are the daffodils?
There were daffodils here last week"—
plaintive, you see, like a dog
who has been given a real cookie just once
and now feels cheated
if he doesn't get them always.

She: "What?—daffodils?
You mean, the *daffodils*?
Well—if you want to wait for them . . ."
(the idea of any idiot
who wanted to wait
for daffodils, growing bigger and bigger in her
smudged eyes). She
gave the cobra-headed mike on the intercom a couple of good whacks
and hollered down the
stacked up wide aisles
we all spend our time in these days
instead of churches,

"Where are the daffodils?"
A lad in a red coat
came onto the scene at the back
like an errand boy who has only happened
to stroll in among the actors
stood there

68

among the shelves full of plastic dishpans,
diapers, foot powder and bandages
trying to remember his right lines,

Daffodils? Did you say daffodils?
as though he thought she wasn't quite
all there.
Time stood still
just waiting,
I thought perhaps the way the old men in the kiva
wait to see if the bean seed
is maybe going to sprout any minute,
the green life
that is meant to keep the world right.

The employee called Betty—
the one they all say when they can't figure it out,
"Ask Betty"—
she suddenly came to
and you could see it click:
"Oh! DAFFODILS! (all in capital letters)
They're in the liquor department!"

Shades of Wordsworth!
who found the daffodils where they were meant to be
and not among the bottles—
What could they be doing there?

I kept on waiting
for anything to happen.
All at once the red-jacketed young man
appeared, bearing a long carton,
set it down on the floor beside the check stand—
nobody paying any attention but me—
He opened the box
and there lay the daffodils.

Oh, explosions and satisfactions!
How Spring had come alive.

Could this be Walgreen's?
Or had time flipped a little
when I happened not to be looking?
I could swear
all the daffodils in the world
swarmed up at me from that
cardboard carton marked Fresh Flowers!
It seemed all at once as though
Juliet had not died,
as though Persephone were found,
or as though it were I
who must have spent all that time among the bottles.

"Spring rides no horses down the hill
nor comes on foot a goosegirl still,"
I reminded Miss Millay whose ghost
by some coincidence had suddenly
showed up.
"Adaptable creature that she is," I told her,
"Spring has just flown out
from Los Angeles by jet plane
in a crowd of golden daffodils,
ice-fresh and unwilted from the greenhouse.
And all the loveliest things there be—if you'll pardon
the expression," I said,
as one poet to another,
"come not so simply as they used to—
but so long as they keep on coming. . . ."
And we smiled at one another from our
different niches in time and space
right under the blank grey eyes of the
toll-collecting mini-goddess,
the red-jacketed youth who didn't know

the part he was really playing,
and a weathered old man who grinned unsurprised through his few teeth,
as though he had been watching goings on like this
forever.

Then I took my seventy-seven
cents worth of daffodils,
my bottle of Kaopectate which in those days was only sixty-five,
and moved offstage to a
chorus of turtles and young lambs. Alleluia!

Biology

On his belly in the dust
serpent goes as serpent must,
sealed forever in this fate
by God's legendary hate;

enemy of God and man,
so they say, since time began,
yet His hand who formed the dew
formed the coiling serpent too;

formed the bird to sing and fly,
formed man's mind to chart the sky,
formed the flower and formed the weed,
formed the serpent to His need.

Microscope at last has shown
in our embryonic bone
bird and man and snake all be
one in common ancestry:

Snake is but, so I have heard,
elder brother to the bird.
Man himself, for all I know,
angel is in embryo.

1950

On Receiving a Bill for Nine Hours of Analysis

She thought: Nine hours is a long time to have gone on talking,
nine hours worth of words.
If placed one end to another how far would they reach?
How many baskets would they fill?
If words were birds,
were toads or diamonds like those girls in the fairy tale,
there'd be a lot by now,
fluttering or hopping or cluttering the floor up,
bursting out the window, rolling down the staircase,
filling the street too, like the sorcerer's apprentice,
no end of words.

Like opening the closets and chests and basement compartments
of an ancestral castle; like Bluebeard's wife
rummaging here and there, obsessed with cleaning
and putting things to rights, shaking the moths out,
setting the caged birds free.
What will she do, I wonder, when she comes to the locked room
and she finds that her little key fits the lock and the door
        will open?
Will she find words for that, I wonder? I wonder will she?
Or will she be mute and let her tell-tale silence betray her
and the windows of her eyes that can never hide what she saw
        there?

1956

The Poet as Big as a Bear

Sits behind the small table shuffling his feet in
shiny new shoes that might have been just bought
for a bear to come out of the woods with.
His enormous round face
is hairy as a bear's except for the bald manskull.
His hands curve
inward like a stuffed bear's paws. He reminds me
of *megatherium* a little,
"an extinct group of
very large sloth-like plant-eating animals
classified as edentate whose remains have been found in
Pleistocene America."
He speaks as a bear might who has swallowed a Harvard professor.
His clothes hang
wrinkled as though he had just crawled out of hibernation.

A strange den for poetry to inhabit, I think, as
out of the round pink cave of his mouth
surrounded by beard-like thickets of underbrush
the words came, the
images crept and flew and
jostled one another as though a
beehive had been broken into
or as though an infant blew sounds like bubbles from
the tip of its pink tongue.
The words swarmed from the womb of his mouth like
creatures that had been hatched there, or
as though he were making an omelet and
seldom got past the stage of opening
the eggs one after another to show us what was inside.
Many of them were infertile, but
some spread marvelous wings and flew forth
in the direction of Mexico.

Others hid among the rafters
of our baffled minds and for all our coaxing
could not be enticed down till long after the hall was emptied.

1957

Catherine and Her Destiny
for Denise Levertov

To haunt a child
lifelong,
this story—
a prism of meanings
each facet, as though beamed from a lighthouse turning
its intermittent shaft.

Was it Destiny's unkindness
or mine?
—the self-persecutions, the
menial service, the ungovernable
tempers, the
linens piled and scattered,
the kind mistresses ill-served?

The story's revelation
that good or ill in one's fate
are mixed
in equal portion,
half lived in the sunlight,
the other lived in shadow.
Catherine did not question
that this must be—
"Six of one, half a dozen of the other,"
as my mother used to say.
But is it true that one can *choose*,
that one has any voice in the allotment?
The fact is
(whether one wills or no)
there is an unequivocal balance
between the dark, the light,
the white keys
and the black.

Climbing the lone mountain
to awaken Destiny
from her long irresponsible slumber—
(But would she not have awakened
anyway in her own time?)
Must there always be
the human effort,
not only the long subjection
but also determined struggle
to reserve what is one's own?

Lear, too, made a bargain with life;
chose (unlike Catherine)
to keep on being happy;
a child with his hand stuffed
deep in the jar of cookies,
had unhappiness heaped upon him
at his life's end,
everything stored up and not lived
"the slings and arrows of fortune"
heaped upon him.
Job, too,
learned the God's other side.

I think poor Catherine
had the best of it
after all,
hardened by sorrow
to withstand final joy.

1971

The Muse

is a spoiled creature
of whose sex and species I am not yet sure.
Since I forced her
to swear off cigarettes she
snacks on cookies;
(cookies make *my* teeth feel gritty
and give me cankers)
but the muse doesn't give a hoot
for *my* comfort or convenience;
will not come when I call her
but at the most inconvenient moment
rushes out of her hiding place and cries,
"Take *this* down,"
not often a subject I myself would have chosen.
Tongue-in-cheek she
strolls in in the morning
like a sloven
while I am making the bed and
contemplating a half-hour with a Mozart sonata,
and as though craving to design
her own self-caricature
demands of me, "Take *this* down,"
which I do, standing at the unopened lid of the piano.

1972

The Poet's World

Sitting here in the morning
half-awake, reclining against pillows,
I look at a notebook of old poems
that my mind barely brushes against.
A wisp of fragrance rises,
a rustle of time, a bare thread of music.

If I read one I will be gathered into a lost land,
a land lying lost within me,
a sudden geography replacing this windowed outlook
of smooth lawn and bushes trimmed neatly by my own hand.

The poet's world
rises in us half-familiar
as a birthplace to which we retrace our steps,
or one that travelers speak of.
The poet does not, as some think, create it,
but makes a form it can fill,
a window this other world looks into.
It longs for habitation, I think, growing tired of shadows
and voices that have no mouths but ours to speak through.

Perhaps I am afraid of this world
that goes echoing within me like a seashell
held at a wondering child's ear,—
a surge of far-off ocean,
kingdoms as lost as Atlantis.
How can one remember
these places one's eye has never looked on
that swarm beneath our eyelids?

If I enter the poem,
if I break off a flower or a single waving
branch, will I be seized by my own roots
and dragged down from the safe surface I walk on
into depths from which return is a mortal struggle
and forever after lamented?

1982

Constellation

Who are we who
seldom if ever
meet?
Perhaps only once in a lifetime
for a day or an hour,
a word on the telephone,
or the brief lifting of masks
at a crowded party.

Who are we whom Time crosses
or whirls for a moment
in the grand right and left
of a round dance?
Who is it calls the figures
in which we meet and part?
What is the gesture of recognition?
Whose colors do we wear
wound in ribbons at our wrist,
or pinned like a green leaf,
or slipped like a bead into a necklace?
How often do we inhabit,
I wonder
each other's dreams?

Do they also journey among us
whose footsteps we sometimes follow
out of a past that goes before us like a beacon?
Is it they who leave writings in stones
we hold in our hands at night,
or in books the wind blows open,
for each of us at a different time
but always at the same page?

Are we all native to another country
or travelers toward one

whose legend we decipher as we journey?
There is a language whose syllables are familiar
yet we cannot speak more than a few words.
How can we tell what we have seen?
Something looks out through our eyes
that may not be spoken.
Though we point together to the same stars
we are often lonely.

Do we all travel, I wonder,
in a single constellation
whose motion cannot be plotted in one lifetime?
The light by which we are sometimes illumined
started far in the future to reach us.
Each of us sees it from a different angle,
or hears notes in a different key.
What is the music, I wonder, that contains us?
What invisible birds fly over
that form and re-form the pattern of the dance
above us?

How distant we always are,
yet time and distance
seem only threads in a net
that does not hold us.
Sometimes another element shines through
we are part of as birds of air
or as fish are of deep water.
In this element
we know and are always known of one another.
Whose is the laughter
runs now and then through the leaves?
What children are playing
forever their blindfold games among us?

1973

What Kind of Old Woman Can I Be?

Great-great grandmaw whom I never knew
died of old age in 1893, age ninety.
The paper said on her 88th birthday
"A witty conversationalist."
Said my mother, the old lady's granddaughter, "She
rocked all day in her little room upstairs,
smoked a corncob pipe, took snuff;
everyday when the children went in to see her,
showed them her treasures over and over."

I would show mine;
perhaps three smooth stones
colored with lines like lost fire,
secret messages, songs imbedded
of mountain headwaters they once knew.

Grandmother Altie Hallett—
her strong conviction that evil and pain were only error,
died at 93, self-divested of every possession,
of whatever human ties had bound her.

Schoolmistress Vida Francis,
tough and passionate for life at 87,
joint-lamed and crutch-dependent,
still traveled wherever she'd a mind to,
leaving letters of love and courage in her lengthening shadow.

Analyst Margaret Nordfeldt,
still analyzing a little when she was 90
in her New York hotel,
around the corner from the Little Carnegie,
and a good restaurant next door,
and a good friend

who often lunched with her.
The two old ladies, giggling, did not scruple
to order and eat the dessert first,
unbound from their lifetimes of propriety.

Or else no one I know:
Perhaps I would be an eccentric
collecting dogs and stray cats
out of the lost and found ads,
"Free kittens." What a temptation!
"Found. Small white ferret with pink eyes."

Old witch who lives in her hut in the forest
with an owl or a toad or such like to do her bidding,
able to change her shape
or travel on a broomstick.

Not
an old woman alone in today's world.

1978

Fragments

I am half in love, sometimes, with my only sister.
She and I have wandered separately
through the worlds of fairy tale.
Everywhere we come upon traces of one another.
We are like two travelers who have made the same pilgrimage
at entirely different times
and who remember together the separate journeys,
the scenes familiar to each, the magic creatures.
Have we not climbed, in our time, the same glass mountain
and worn out the same iron shoes
seeking to rescue our lost loves from the false princess?
There have been dragons along the way
but always, and in unexpected places,
helpers.
Always and over and over have we not both been learning
to embrace the Beast we have shunned
and tried to deny within us?

The end of the journey always brings recognition;
the old witch's power is ended.
Whichever one thought herself the ugly sister,
whichever the despised princess,
knows she was neither.
They were only shadows of one another.

1980

Perhaps in Our Old Age

Perhaps in our old age
we can return again to being children,
return to our playful places,
to the magic world we were once part of;
to the roots of old trees where the gnomes delved
and hid their secret treasure;
to the fairy wand that could transform us;
to the finger dipped in the cauldron
and the language of birds understood then;
to the shoes of swiftness and the cap of darkness;
to the game of horse thieves;
to Dapplegrim our great steed
who helped the lad win a kingdom
and a princess;
to the well where the maiden dropped her spindle
and fell after it into a fairy realm.
Perhaps in our old age
we can find that well again and lean above it
and behold our own long lost treasure.

Let us unearth our childhood
like a bone hidden and long forgotten
by an old dog, and gnaw the marrow of it
and bring the taste back again
of those times when our imaginations ran free
and every straight stick became a pony
and our real ponies steeds of fire.
Let us take hands and re-enter the loved stories
as though we were children running from a schoolroom
into a world we long ago lost and longed for,
that waits for us still at the far edge of dreaming,
a world where the wicked witch is at last outwitted,
where the shining birch tree
drops gold and silver blessings on the true bride.

1982

Construction

I saw in my dream last night
a lean dog dragging squared lumber up a hillside:
two-by-fours made of redwood, one shorter than the other,
cut by a careful carpenter who knew in his mind's eye
exactly the angle they should fit together.
The dog had a nonchalant look as though thieving were his hobby
whether or not it had any useful purpose;
just indulging his instinct made him happy.
I watched him lug the lumber
into a shed-like machine shop and hide it under
the rusted wreck of an old car
the way a dog in the wild will drag part of his kill
back to his den and worry it at his leisure.

When I woke I found myself thinking of the poet, Neruda,
who works on a poem, he says, like a carpenter.
First he chooses the wood for its fragrance and its color,
its smoothness and its resonance with deep forests.
Next he saws into the board until the sparks fly;
from the sections he makes his verses.
The poem begins to take shape like the hull of a stout ship
exultant to ride soon on the moon-heaped waters.

I too feel
that poetry and construction have much in common.
For a lifetime I have been dragging home stray boards
that I hoped my poems or my house might someday have a use for;
scraps left over from finished houses;
beachcombed remnants of old wrecks,
a few smoothed pieces of fine wood
that a cabinet maker couldn't find a use for;
the growth of the tree in its grain still sings
like fragments of torn music.

There is a longing in old wood to find its meaning
again in being part of something
before its essence returns to earth
or before fire
gives it back once more to air.

Remember when we were children the smell of shavings,
the curls from a planed board,
the smoothed board
balanced over a log to make a see-saw?
The notched board we loosely hung to complete our rope swing?
Remember the stilts we made from the sawmill discards,
the stick horses we galloped on,
even the random chips that became boats
knife-carved to race on our flowing summer water?

We gathered the scraps of whatever was cast off around us
to furnish our own bare space,
half imitation, half fluent imagination.
How could we let anything lie that held promise of becoming?
How could our hands deny the urge for making
that possesses all human kind?
A dog can twitch in his dream and
run after the rabbit till he wakes.
Only we humans
can make houses or poetry or music
out of the stuff poets say all dreams are made on.

1982

Lines for a Woman Poet
for May Sarton

What do I know about your human life?
Upon your shoulder sits a bird and sings.
I know that bird. I know that falcon eye,
those beating wings that drive it toward the sun,
the whirling plunge of light and the curved beak
and how it tears the heart to drink the blood,
the living blood on which its song must feed.

I share being woman with you and I know
the god's indifference to our mortal pain.
Daphne who terrified became a tree
and Leda stretched beneath the dazzling wings
cried against violation as we cry.
After the blaze of light the dark comes down
and we must go, still human and alone
into the nine months' night that forms the child,

into the dark like Cora with her song
and with her broken flowers still in her hand
to die like summer back into the earth
from which all summers spring. We cannot soar
like birds toward the sun. We must endure
the weight of winter and the darkened moon,
not like Van Gogh who was devoured by light
until his brush bled fire.

Let the fierce phoenix go with his sharp cry
toward the flaming sun, oh mythical bird
that would consume your heart. Lie down, lie down
now among roots and leaves and let your eyes
be dark as the closed child's and let the mole
speak his blind wisdom to your folded hand.
Birth is not had by willing. Let the rose
unfurl, in time like air, what summer knows.

1959

PART
THREE

This Dancing
Ground of Sky

I Have Looked at the Earth

And you said: I am afraid to have you fly.
Had you forgotten that afternoon on Point Lobos
When, because the tide of centuries that had swept over
    those rocks somehow washed over us with the sound
    of unceasing water, and because there was so much
    life there in the color of tree-shadowed sky and voices
    invisible and not human,
We said that the more we could be aware of the world,
    of the color and sound of it, of its taste in our mouths
    and the feel of it under our fingers,
The more we could perhaps remember and recognize and
    regain of its beauty
After death had stripped us of our familiar tools for seeing
    and listening and touching?
We thought, for the space of an afternoon, with the
    thought of rocks. The deep heart of the earth,
    muffled and unhurried, sounded through us. We al-
    most took root there, forgetting we were human and
    mortal, becoming earth there at the sea's edge.

When we are dead we know this one thing will become
    of us:
We will go into the ground; our bodies will surely
    crumble and feed tree-roots, or blow as dust on the
    wind or be rain-washed at last into ocean.
Is it this you fear for me, bidding me not fly, bidding
    me go carefully and save this body?

If there were any more danger in flying than always in
    living, when death hangs ever invisible above our
    heads, and we never know at what instant the
    thread will be cut that holds it,

Would it be so dreadful to drop, in an interval of ecstasy,
     in a fear-escaping second, out of this human exist-
     ence, to go back to earth and be one in the constel-
     lations, to give birth to mountains, to be intimate
     with the tide and the rain and the seasons?

I have known these moments of unlimited happiness:
That afternoon on Point Lobos that was like going home
     out of an alien country;
A moment on Tsacoma Mountain where the tides of the
     air are shattered like waves and become clouds, and
     go down as rain on the sea-forgotten valley;
And that moment of flying over the Mojave. The pain
     of death at that moment would not have been greater
     than my heart bore at beholding earth naked and
     virgin with the shadow of twilight above her like
     a lover.
Each of these moments was like a sudden dying, a brief
     escape from the body, an instant of being the beauty
     which, living, we only taste a little.
Oh never fear death for me for I have looked at the
     earth and loved it. I have been part of earth's beauty
     in moments beyond the edge of living.

Sketchbook

March 14, 1972

A red and blue kite
lashed to the highest branch
of a chinese elm
hung there for now seven days
has turned to a pale ghost
the skeleton of a last year's leaf
or the cast-off husk
of an old moon.

March 16

Spring comes
a smug cliché of fat buds
the earth is getting ready
to spring spring upon us
the birds are making a racket
in the bland air
Why do I growing old
in all this abundance of life
say to death, Move over;
Let us sit together a moment
on the doorstep?

March 18

A woman reads
the Wayside Garden Catalogue
in her seventieth year,

And sighs.
She knows she must not yield to the temptation.
What she plants now

Will not be of this world,
Will not be for her to delight in,
will belong to another dimension
of time than can be measured
by years and familiar seasons.

She must surrender the dream of another fragrant lilac
under her window,
the sweet-scented syringa
the carpet of rose red thyme,
the hedge of white scotch roses
she somehow never got round to.

She must learn to content herself—oh difficult lesson,
with what is and not what might be,
knowing her strength no longer equal
to rearrangement.

Foretaste

The day stood up around me, blue,
Farther than sight, and then I knew
The river was a blue track curled
Through the pale center of my world.
The mountains leaned against the sky,
Blue piled on blue, immensely high,
And in the sky a slant-winged bird
Moved slowly, like a singing word.
Onward I drove and saw the road
Unwind blue miles; the river flowed
Implacable and strong and wide,
Lifting pale waves, a hurrying tide,
And trees grew up along its brim
And higher towered the mesa's rim,
Drawing a black, unbroken line
Across blue sky as clear as wine,
So clear I almost saw a star,
Bright as infinity, and far.

I was not body-bound this day.
The mountains pulled me clear away.
Upward I burned like their blue flame;
Then turned my eyes and quickly came
In one short flight to colored hills
Where no leaf grows. The black rain spills
Out of fierce clouds on silver days
And carves steep earth in curious ways.
And then I lay, a sage-swept plain,
Slanting to riverward again.

I held low houses on my breast
And wide church doors that opened west.
With simple folk I knelt and prayed,
And in their bodies long I stayed.

With their own hands I shaped warm earth
To bricks, and in swept rooms gave birth
To many a child, and saw some die.
I felt my breasts grow old and dry.
My tear-spent eyes were deep and wise
And sorrowless as star-edged skies.
At last I died and became earth
Close to the house that saw my birth.

And suddenly this curious thing:
Like spinning earth I seemed to sing.
A spinning earth I then became
And whirled through space like a clear flame.
Mountains were part of me, and then
Made of the same flame I knew men.
Oh then I saw what death might be,
What keen, unfettered ecstasy
To be the earth, not just to see
Blue light spilled over hill and tree;
To feel the rain tread on my heart,
Not watch it shine, a thing apart;
And in all men to be the fire
Of grief and joy and swift desire.

My car moved slow. I felt the road
Weigh down upon me like a load.
I saw a woman brown of face
Hoeing hard earth with strong, sure grace.
I looked at her as at my friend.
I saw her turn from me and bend
Over her work. She did not know
I'd worn her flesh a while ago.
She did not even hear my cry.
Prisoned in body now was I.
I looked out on the gathering stars
As though my eyes were prison bars.

Peach Trees

Do not hurry past this orchard too quickly
Saying: Yes, surely, that is a beautiful thing.
As though the moment of flaming were the
    purpose of this orchard
Accomplished now that your all-claiming eyes
    have seen it.
Remember that before these trees were ever planted,
A thin, small, unprotesting beast of burden
Dragged a curved plough through the reluctant earth,
With a man stooping behind in the hot sun to
    guide it.
Remember a wide ditch had to be dug here
    to coax the river
Up the dry, stubborn flanks of these hills, a
    long time barren,
And that a woman, ageless as the brown
    hills are ageless,
Hoed the difficult earth about the young roots planted,
And dreamed, before ever the slender branches
    had budded,
Of yellow fruit spread to the sun in her dooryard
    in autumn.

After the Rain

After the rain the earth lies back in sunlight,
her lovely limbs relaxed, her breasts quiescent,
her long hair spread upon the wind like perfume.
After the rain the earth becomes a woman
a lover can lie at peace with, becomes a woman
who holds in her hands the weightless arch of the rainbow.
She lies with her eyes half-closed. She lies half-dreaming.
She lies like a swimmer half-submerged in sunlight.

This Ocean (Point Lobos)

All day we watched the ocean
heaping its white, incredibly brief blossoms
over the agony-veined, dark granite:
all day the green sea-water
thrusting into the rock clefts.

Seals basked,
barking at tide's edge,
swam, elusive as thought,
under the fluid marble
surface of deep water.

Cypress
more ancient than memory
absorbed us into shadow.

I saw dead girls
bruise their white breasts
on the indifferent rock,
sea-sharpened, crystal, harder than diamond:
their long hair
netted the pale tide.

Darkness came down:
the gaunt sea-vultures
roosted, red-beaked
in the bleak rock.

I dared not touch you
with word or weight of finger:
your own gods claimed you, the elemental granite
bare at your heart's core.

Now I must take this ocean
into my own heart or be taken by it,
going down into it, naked and voiceless and
torn by the rocks like the drowned girls.

Familiar Journey

Back and forth on the same road
and the same hills.
I and the seasons going back and forth
on the same road; the orchards blossoming,
ripening their fruit, and the harvest gathered.
A new house is built and an old one
crumbles. In the late nights
one window is sometimes lighted.
Who watches in silence
while an old man dies or a child is being born?
I and the stars go past
again and again on the same road.

The dark nights and the bright ones,
the summer days
with the clouds blossoming above the mountains,
tremendous flowers, white, and sheathed in purple
like the flowers of yucca;
and the meadow larks
with a song as cool as the fields of green alfalfa;
the cottonwood tree
at the curve of the ditch near Pojoaque
where the old men sit all day
and the young girls at night with their lovers,
the old tree that remembers
more than the oldest man in that village remembers
and that dies slowly now, withdrawing its shadow
a little every year.

And the luminous valley
where nothing grows but color,
blues, lavenders, violets,
and all the shades of rose seen in a sunset;

the long bluff like a wave,
a wave the color of a cloud at sunset,
a wave that never breaks,
transfixed forever at the moment of its breaking,
and the sharp spires like the bending crest of the wave;
the hills that go naked always to the sun,
naked to starlight,
clothing themselves in no shadow,
the remnants of ancient valleys,
fragments of canyon walls the wind and weather
have not destroyed yet,
secret valleys
only the sun and the wind know.

I going back and forth on the same road
as if it were another body that contained me;
and the great storms, the afternoons of sunlight,
the dark nights,
the mountains that are a flame on one horizon,
and the mountains like a blue, an incandescent shadow
rimming the west;

Familiar journey,
and the years of a life,
the happenings of a life
along this road like remembered hills,
like the valleys.

Enchanted Mesa

Hard to climb:
the slow talus
yielding under the bent step:
the cleft in the rock where
the wind leaps
upward like chill flame:
swallows screaming.

Earth's weight
drags at the belly.
The heart soars.
Torn between
earth and clean air
we hang
clenched in hard rock.

Hand over hand now:
the blood roars
in the reluctant throat veins.
Do not look downward
onto the warm plain,
the level, the acquiescent
safe earth.

These perpendicular
weather-fractured cliffs of
sandstone intercept the
sharp sky.
The complacent
mind drags at the winged heel.

But the bright edge
finally triumphs.
We stand fast,
erect in wind's path.
The waves of
time beat on the
sheer rock.

Swallows protest our coming,
go past us like
arrows from a tense bow,
curved flight,
cleaving wind with
their sharp cries.

An hour on this
mesa escapes time.
Humanity vanishes,
becomes an unheard procession
on remote roads. Only the strong
skeletal firmness of earth holds
sky on its shoulders.

Holds us also
that which we strove against
in climbing.
The heart soars
lifted upon its own roots.
Enchanted Mesa—
a winged rock rooted in the
spent plain.

Autumn Dusk

Over the hill's dark edge
the road curves.
Yellow gathers like a cloud at the bend beyond the river,
rushes toward us up the roadside.

Color of trees, autumnal, moving in a new dimension,
forward in space, and the wave breaks as the car leaps through it.
The oiled ribbon of dark road
unwinds in yellow margins.

Motion of machinery,
hurrying pistons in rhythmical vertical descension,
wheel circumference revolving on the hard road.
The season draws its slow arc on the earth's shell.
The arc of sunset
widens like a stain in the pale sky.

Oh luminous evening
cleft at the core like a silver knife through a fruit's heart,
the two halves opening backward.
The core is motionless,
is speed quiescent at the heart of motion.
We move like an arrow bearing our swiftness with us.
The moon comes up out of last light and follows us slowly.

Horses in the Moonlight

In the morning I found that no one had seen them,
no one had wakened and heard them, the beautiful horses,
shaking the moonlight from their flanks like water,
silver in their long manes, silver in their bright tails,
their hooves as brittle as glass ringing on the light snow.

I opened the doors. I called my companions: come quickly
    and see them,
the horses dancing in the moonlight, the live, the beautiful
    horses.
But no one heard me. Buried under a hundred coverlets of
    deep sleep
my brother, my companion, my beloved
all lay sleeping, lay sleeping and would not listen.

Sleep and do not look on this strange scene, my lords and
    masters,
lest you feel them clearing the careful fences of your own
    minds,
possessing your unaccustomed hearts in breathtaking beauty,
and a wildness your hand cannot tame
and a strength your knees can never master.

Here Is Ground Juniper

Here is ground juniper the which to find
we followed where November snowfall, quietly cherished
lay unravished by sun or wind in steepest canyon
    shadowed by rock walls

and by the laced fingers of a thousand fir trees
all day weaving sun and wind into silence,
all day spreading an impenetrable web of twilight
    over that canyon.

Ground juniper grows among roots and boulders
and close to mountain rivers. Like an eye dreaming
the water shines between snowbanks. It moves like molten
    gold over dark leaf.

We walk quietly and brush snow-cover from juniper.
The branches spring forth, live and tinted with silver,
bearing along their stem the shy and infrequent
    dusk-colored berry.

Oh strangest and loveliest of evergreens,
semi-sepulchred beneath snowfall, winter-imprisoned
upon earth's sleeping heart, green and undying
    witness of life and summer.

Morning on Tseregé

When I was a child I climbed here
at sunrise, barefooted among the grasses.
I searched for arrowheads among the ruins
and stood wondering on the rims of the broken kivas.
I had no language to say what it was that moved me,
the voiceless communication that thundered all about me,
a wisdom of rocks and old trees, of buried rivers,
of the great arcs and tangents of sky and mountain,
and always the grass that whispered upon the ruins
where a people had lived and fought, had died and had been
     forgotten.

They had left drawn on the rocks, their suns, their serpents,
and scattered among the dust, the broken potsherds
with their symbols of cloud, of rain, of the eagle flying.
And so without words I knew that man is mortal
and doomed both to live and to die, but what he worships
     lives on forever.

Today with my own world crumbling toward ruin
I know this still, and I greet the child who will stand here
upon Tseregé and watch the morning blossom
and feel under her questioning hand, the living grasses
weaving substance of sunlight and the dust of a fallen city.

Blue Heron

At the place where the canyon is wide and the river is shallow
and the sandbars are thick with cottonwood and rosy willow
I, driving around a bend in the road, and the world still in shadow,
    with my own eyes suddenly saw the blue heron fishing.

I was going too fast then to stop. The sun had not risen.
The river was quiet and without color as a crystal prism
that has not caught light yet, and the heron was half-hidden
    in a background of bare branches, yet I saw him fishing

immobile as though he had been rooted there forever
among the willows, long legs stretched and limber,
the serpentine neck poised, sheathed in quiescent feather,
    the live eye aware of the sky, and the road and the fish in the river.

Not moving, nor pursuing, but waiting in that stillness,
in the calm of the morning before the voices of children
shattered the air like glass, and men were driven
    against time and none could remember the blue heron fishing.

1950

Black Mesa: Dream and Variations

1.

In a twilight of rain
the mesa gathered her robes around her,
veils of mauve and blown smoke,
colors of dark cloud lined with a buried sunset.

The mountain, the Black Mesa,
loomed suddenly before us like a ghost ship,
a figment of clouds and torn sails
gone aground out of time,
cast up out of a never-existing ocean.
No seacoast welcomed her,
only the bare hills and a desert river.
What resonance of waters,
what urge in clouds and in stone to take form
in a reflecting eye had seized us
to be its collaborators?
The Black Mesa
waked an old legend in us, tales of a black ship
or a ship with black sails we could only half-remember,
an alien dream projected from a past world
through our rapt eyes
on the curtain of rain and darkness.

2.

On this afternoon of vision
they were dancing the Turtle Dance at San Ildefonso
in a medley
of shells and green boughs.
Left alone
for an hour on the other side of the river,
closed in by a slow rain,
I slept in the labyrinth of myself.

I went down through the vertical corridors of heaped time
with their indelible graffiti
their coiled and unascended music
down to the melt of the world and the unformed crystal essence
that would someday blossom and reflect light.
I listened at the root of the Black Mesa
like an attached child
that hears only its own and its mother's heartbeat.

3.

The mesa,
alert to the sound of the drum and of strung shells,
of ascending male voices,
guarded her mystery
in cinders and slow crystals,
in a mantle of river stones,
in the sloped debris of worn hills,
in facets of retained light.

Monument to earth's fire,
the melt of her inwardness:
unnamed gods came surging
forth from the womb's dark.
Taking light in their hands as they rose
they wove it like a vestment
over hills wrinkled with time,
over stones long abandoned by their rivers.

4.

Landmarked center of a universe,
terrestrial axis,
still body at the center of time's motion,
I have watched morning and evening revolve around you,
heard the seasonal birds fly over,
handled the washed stones,
looked down on you from the stretched rim of mountains

113

at the valley's either side.
Always you drew my wandering gaze toward you
from whatever height I leaned on.
From each direction I saw the light drain downward
seeking to fill your dark well.
You are a lodestone,
compact essence of extinct fire,
a hand reaching
out of earth's whirling depth to seize light
and make yourself its darker habitation.

5.

Black Mesa,
hard core from which a landscape
has been eaten away by rainfall and a river.
Washed gravels at rest above earth's tilt
lie level as instruments among the torn hills,
anatomy of an island or an altar.
Oceans of light wash round her.
The Black Mesa devours light
like a collapsed star,
drawing it down into the dark shaft
from which her substance fountained.
Leaning columns of black rock
intrude shadow
like bars of upright music.
Only the pale grass at the surface shines
softly in winter,
a platform raised for the feet of holy dancers.

6.

The river levels the land around the mesa.
Sleek as an animal, muscular as serpents,
it is bearing our world away.
The river's aim is only to flow onward;
the mesa's to remain.

Among the stars and seasons
she keeps her fixed place.
Though the earth moves beneath her,
though the mountains perish,
she is rooted too deep to tremble.
She has been through it all before.
She will still be here when the hills crumble
and are heaped along a no longer living
river.
When the drums fall silent
who will they be who someday come to dream her
into themselves again?

White Dog with Mushrooms

On a smoothed-off hilltop
among the granite outcrops
I am sitting this December morning
observing among the random
and wrinkled stones at the base of a
juniper a colony of mushrooms
with caps the color of warm toast.

No bigger in circumference
than a dime and most of them
smaller, they are
gathered in clusters like a
game of jackstones,
or like stars on the sphere
of a child's eye.

The sky is pale blue; the wind
like an invisible herd with horns in velvet
goes butting among the rough trees.
My skin rejoices
in the warm prick of winter,
warmth and cold joined
like a pair of
lively dancers.

The white dog, Poli-kota,
runs on spiraling errands in her loose flesh.
She is a collector of footprints,
of urinal smells draped over
bushes and low tree branches.
Her curled tongue
delivers damp messages
to my cold cheek.

She is unmindful of mushrooms,
treads them down blindly
in a quadruple disaster.
My heart cries
to think what like death
may someday befall our planet,
not anyone's purpose,
no one will mean to do it,
something random to us
as Poli among the mushrooms.

Still on this hillside
where dying and coming to life
go hand in hand together
I cannot mind long.

Here is a bone I have found,
perhaps a steer's vertebra
once hidden in gliding flesh.
Now weathered and whitened
it lies in my hand
like a wordless metaphor
in the shape of a butterfly.

On the Putting to Death of an Old Dog

Put to death:
The words we used were
"put to sleep,"
but sleep is not the same thing
as death.
In sleep the breath comes and goes still.
Under the eyelids dreams flicker;
the paws twitch
at intervals with a running motion.
When I watched you sleeping near me
I knew that life was living in you.
Your senses would vibrate in dreaming
like the tuned strings of an instrument.
Your still form stretched out
was filled with some purpose
remote from my human world.
It was as though you traveled
trails you had never seen
yet familiar as you dreamed them.
Did the arctic wastes of your origin
wake in you?
Did you follow the scent, perhaps,
of a snowshoe rabbit
through a far white winter landscape?
You were running free of the leash now,
free of the restraining world of humans.

I recall how on the trail when I rested
you would come to my side a moment
and then withdraw
to contemplate wilderness after your own fashion,
ears sifting the air for the least rustle
of bird's wing or of insect,
nose sniffing the language of worlds I could not enter.

When I slept in the noon shade you would roam a little
but never too far.
Something bound you to me
stronger than wild ancestral yearnings.
I forced you to obey me,
to keep your place always,
to suppress your exuberance
for the sake of domestic calm;
yet your leaps of wild ecstasy
stirred Dionysus in my own blood.
Sometimes by mountain water
I would feel my heart start beating
to the sound of a long forgotten music.

When you grew old
and your senses were fast failing
the veterinary surgeon
put you to sleep
and death.
It was a simple operation.
I kept my hands on you all the time.
You could no longer hear me,
the voice of command, the voice of reassurance,
the voice of love
and at last of separation.
How often my words had calmed you on the same high table,
trembling as all dogs do
at the probing fingers,
the preventive inoculations.
It seemed strange
that this time you did not flinch when the anesthetic needle
went in,
nor draw back when the tube like a slender serpent
found the vein through which death must enter.
It seemed as though you withdrew of your own free will
and shut the last door between us.

For a moment you lay outstretched in your warm fur,
warm under my hands that rested on you,
warm as though sleeping near me on your house rug
or bedded in winter sunlight on the white snow:
then in one single instant
gone;
as though someone had thrown a master switch
and the world's machinery silenced,
no more light,
nothing that could receive warmth
from the touch of a warm hand.

The life surging through you, in one eye's blink
vanished
without a trace or an echo.
Whatever in you had dreamed
was gone too.
Nothing remained
but this complete cessation,
and I, an old woman, clutching at a dream's end
wordless in the steep shadow
of my own death.

Elegy for the Willow Tree

The willow tree in the garden
died back a little more each year.
Her long hair of green leaves,
each tear-shaped like the mark of a star on exposed film,
shortened and became thin.

She stood at the edge of the lawn like a witch in tatters
bereft of her youthful magic.
The knobs of her weathered bones showed through
and the cicatrices
of shed branches and amputations.
Her pose became awkward like that of an aged dancer
who can no longer keep up with the strong music
that summer and the winds weave.

I said to the man with the chain saw and the ladder,
"Let us now grant her a quick death.
Let the place where she stands be empty.
Let the birds take their song elsewhere.
Let us wipe our sky clean forever of this sad shape."

All afternoon I watched the branches falling
and winced in my deepest bone to hear the rough saw
cut through the rings of time.
Did those shudders, I wonder, spread downward among the clenched roots
and the choked-off fountains of dark water?
Did pain run quivering through earth's finest fibres?
Trembling I hid from the sound of that execution.

When I came out the green branches had been hauled off.
Only the rough trunk still stood
at the edge of the lawn like a monument.
A few handfuls of live green

were all that still trembled on the blank air.
And my heart wept for the lost golden presence,
for the circumference of shadow,
for the vertical strands of green music,
the long drooping arpeggios.

This tree was its own world.
It was alive with motion and with being.
Its leaves were a whirl of stars.
From now on what will the birds do?
the spiders who moored their webs here?
sunlight that traveled so far to become substance?

Oh what can I do to salvage a remnant of beauty
from beauty's dismemberment?
How can I tempt the rainbow
colors of summer to keep on dancing round her?
a wild clematis to wash its white stars over
like the froth of a blown wave?
or a thicket of aspen to lift a new green music
out of the rotted roots?

In time past my wish might have made a goddess of her
and hung the truncated form with offerings,
baskets of fruit and garlands, a cage of songbirds,
a harp out of Babylon.
Now I can only let her
go free to her un-becoming.
Under my feet the hungry earth is waiting
with its many-mouthed creatures to taste this sacrament.
Oh earth, air, water, fire!
Oh essence of bright summer!
I stand on the threshold of what mysteries?

Return to a Landscape
for Mary McArthur Bryan

1.
Around the mountain,
backward into a world behind time,
landscape expanding like a dream,
like rings that widen and vanish across water.

All this world had been water once
and mountains crumbled,
washed down to form plains that still hold the form of water,
hills rounded and rippled like a moving ocean,
grass in the wind making the motion of water.
Ahead of us black ridges like a seacoast
where the tides of wind race upward
and shatter against the unswerving walls of black rock,
black rock that was fluid once
and retains the sharp memory of fire.

Oh these are plains
that summon something like music to a man's blood,
a surge, a deep-sea swelling.
Doors open within him on a far space
broken only by morning and evening.
A feeling of wildness
knocks at his unaccustomed heart.
It is as though a released bird
remembered the use of wings.
The sloping grasslands
waken ancient nomadic dreams.
Visions of grazing herds begin to shimmer;
the horseman wakens;
a sudden rhythm of riding
pulses at wrists and knees.
Oh limitless space! Oh brightness
of clear air!

Out of the youth leaps a manhood
like the sword from encasing stone.
A new land awaits him with its unborn legends,
its challenge, its trials of strength.
He has bidden his fathers farewell.
The voices of cautionary women
call after him ever more faintly and without answer.

Born of such men, you and I,
exuberant children
whose fathers, half in playfulness, half earnest,
put bridles into our hands and taught us to gallop
with the wind and the sun and the power of a strong horse running;
taught us before we knew writing and spelling
to clasp the leather saddle with our firm knees,
to speak with our hands through relaxed reins,
to feel the animal's spirit part ours
and ours the horizon-seeking mind that was wholly human.

Now we, two aging women,
wrenched from this land before our youth was over,
still feel the imprint of its seasons
like rings that mark a tree's growth.
Strangers to one another through half our lifetime
we share no kinship,
no ancestral memories unite us
yet
closer than kinship
the current of earth's music that flows through us.
At the end of our separate pilgrimage
we come together in time's single focus
and mingle our memories.

It is these men, our fathers, whose blood moves in us,
old women that we now are.
We who have borne our own children
and seen them grown and gone,

stand here at the rim of our spent childhood
when we were still half-girl, half-boy.
Woman's strict destiny had not claimed us;
distance enchanted us;
rough trails like an unspoken language
were ours to decipher daily:
this way the shod or the cleft hoof
passed, the print of the predator
crossed here. Above us the storm clouds
threatened and drove us at a gallop
ahead of rainfall back to safe roofs and our warm walls,
back to the rancher's homeplace
that for children was all joy.
We knew nothing then of its difficult dimension,
the wrestling with losses and dry seasons,
maternal terrors,
a woman's troubled dreams of her children's future
and the long loneliness.

The women, my mother and yours,
endured for the men's sake.
They quieted themselves with gardens and with sewing.
I still wear my mother's silver thimble
that was her grandmother's before;
when I prick my finger
the drop of blood is theirs.

My mother sewed flowered curtains
to make her room a bower.
She made no concession at all to wilderness.
Would not meet it even halfway—
she who in childhood rode her grandfather's tall horses,
the least motion of her hands exacting obedience.
Her childhood love of wildness withered in her,
a promise blighted
before the too early blossom could set fruit.

I think she never
forgave the uncaring land.

How did we come by our unmothered love of bare hills
that grew strong in our lives like a wide-spreading tree
outweathering all our weathers?
What stirring of once known springs and waters
urges us to return like birds that migrate
in response to a slant of light?
We wandered all day on roads that only you remembered,
yet familiar as my own dreams.

2.

Toward the end of the glowing afternoon
we came to the cemetery
half an unplanted mile past the waning town.
The dark bulk of the Wagonmound shelters it,
a shape imagined
in the light-dazed eyes of waterless travelers.
Now the lapsed tides of history have left it stranded
like the wraith of a beached ship.
Only the dust long years ago compacted
by the struggling wagonwheels remembers,
and the bones of the dead who lived in the shadow of its legend.

"That cemetery that wants to be a poem," my notes say,
"from Greek *Kometerion*, a sleeping place":
a sleeping place out of doors
as though trail-weary travelers
had thrown their blankets down on the bare earth
and made the sky their roof—
a long night watch
and the bright familiar stars;
by day the striding sun,
cloud shadows, rainfall,
herds in far distance moving,
an eagle in rings of flight.

The dead are resting here in weathered silence.
The same grass waves over them that waves on the plain beyond;
the feathered seed stems
are printed on light like the notes of composed music
a score waiting the wind's touch.
Unswayed by any wind the marble gravestones
defy mortality. More resistant to time than mountains
they will become dust
long after the shape of the Wagonmound is forgotten.
The polished gray surfaces
do not blend with the sloped land;
their squared shapes are dissonant.
Light flows around them
like waves around tidal markers.
As we stand together by your father's graveplot
the high winds of autumn blow over us.
Far off the cattle herds are moving
to their seasonal destination.
Cloud shadows scud
across the rippled hills.

Like children studying a primer
we lean closer to read the straight-ruled biographies
imprinted on each stone:
a name, a birthdate, the year in which a life ended;
a few curt numbers,
all that remain to mark the little space
in measureless time these lives filled.
Your father died too young, still in achieving midlife
when his children were not half-grown.
Much later your mother returned to lie beside him
in final companionship;
nothing to tell of how they lived together,
endured the land or loved it.

The home ranch
has passed into other hands.
No one of your name now
rides the long fences or
counts the drifting lines of cattle or
watches the sky for blessing or threat of rainfall.
Only this narrowed space of earth remains
out of all he once called his own—
all that had once seemed yours
as in childhood my father's acres
seemed mine, my storybook, my
horizon-bounded playground.
Today I envied your heritage
of this little length of ground,
your right, when you die, to be part of it
which perhaps you will never claim.

Why does it seem to matter
to some of us, I wonder,
with what dust our bones are mingled?
Your father sleeps here
with his life absorbed into the land's silence;
mine far away in the city he thought he had escaped from.
It was a possessive sister
who on his death retrieved the prodigal
and consigned his reluctant ashes to the cold tomb.
Did the released spirit, I wonder,
find its own way back among the lights and shadows
to the high plains he loved?
without bones or mortal body
to be borne as in dream to the place of his dream's emergence?

Women have seen men lose their hearts to landscape.
My father did; and yours, more fortunate,
won a livelihood. In death he was not exiled.
The woman beside him, your mother,

would have preferred to lie at the roots of roses
with a green lawn over her.
What can she do with so much empty space,
no great trees to cast shadow
between her and the naked sun?

My own mother
grew intolerant of wide vistas.
After my father's death she built a new house with high windows
and shut the mountain out.
She who in her school days played Rosalind
let Rosalind die in her, denied the forest
and armored herself in duty.
She hid the gypsy girl's wistful picture
an no longer sang us ballads.

Sometimes I remember
with a pang in my heart how she once tried to teach me
in a brimming darkness edged with pine trees
the names of the bright stars and the constellations,
the Lyre, the Swan, the Sword of Perseus.
For her the night sky gleamed with heroes.
The horseman she married ran away from dragons.
After the children came he insisted on remaining
only a laughing child still.
He used the land for his plaything. She became housebound.
The swift-footed mare he gave her was never again saddled.

I, her firstborn,
molded feature on feature in her own likeness,
grew up with a different nature.
The first air I breathed was the midnight air of a canyon
cleft in these same wide plains.
Wherever I went I carried its imprint in me
as the fish to deep water the mark of its spawning ground.
When I die I would like to return to this earth that made me

and be part once more of its substance,
the smallest crystal
that still holds the memory of a human lifetime
in a minute circuitry. Whatever my reaching senses
have touched
becomes one with the resonance of rock,
with the underground whisper of sunken waters,
with magnetic currents
that roots and the smallest insects are aware of.
I carry a cell in which all I have seen lies folded,
mountains and oceans and storm clouds,
mineral color and the color of light reflected
in stone and in waterdrop.
The air I have breathed will someday be shaped into another music.

As I stood beside you in the graveyard
I felt memory throb within us.
Our young days were not lost.
The life we had taken hold of
was conformed to the shape of our hands;
in each whorl of a fingertip,
each braided line of our palms, the feel of our lives still lingered.
Our eyes have netted this land with lines of beauty.
Whatever once stirred in us will go on singing.

Do the dead, I wonder, listen?
Does an essence linger
that is sentient still to music?
Will the grass springing over us absorb our dreaming
and scatter it among birdcalls?

Autumn: Ranchos
November 1st

The grey sky
thickens above the mountain.
The smoke blows
like warning banners, northward instead of east.
The barometer
needle sinks, the geese have flown
south long ago.
Fires burn
furiously up their chimneys;
leaves fall slow;
they whisper conspiracy.
The cattle turn
in resignation toward the wild
plum and the willow thickets.
Birds confer
along the swinging wires
in ruffled rows.
An old man
hurries his sheep across the sullen hill.
Will he make it home, I wonder
before it snows?

1944

For a Mountain Burial

A granite ridge:
the mountain's firm crust
once fluid
become stone.
We buried her
under the low-bending branch of a fir tree,
all that was left
after the final burning,
her bodily remains
reduced as much as possible
to ash.

Some of it drifted in a fine veil
on the light cloudy wind;
the rest we mingled
with granite particles
and leaf-mold,
and I thought of the tree
drawing its mineral nourishment
from bone cells
and crumbled granite.

Let rain's dark music
dissolve her elements;
we leave her to the mountain mists and waters,
forgetting the long struggle not to die,
cleansing out memories
of the last traces of possession.
Let no one now strive to keep her
captive to any mind
or heart-formed image.
May all ghosts take the form of birds
and begin singing
among the birds of daybreak.

Outing in the Wilderness

Blake built Jerusalem
among the Satanic mills of England;
never saw this mountain wilderness;
never saw Jerusalem either,
only watched it in his special mirror.
For him Heaven's gate was built there.
He gave us the clue which following
we might enter.

The rainbow
moves as we move.
There is a pot of gold
at the end of it. I,
though knowing better,
still wistfully believe this.

Another mysterious question:
Can there be sound if there is no ear to hear it?

I muse as we drive along;
the little obedient auto
seems to find its own way
around these curves;
my hands feel for it,
leaving the mind free.

Autumn is
trembling on the verge.
The aspens are turning already;
a wash of watercolor yellow
drips down among the ice blue
cone-candled spruce trees.

"This is the time of year when skunks
like to come down among the houses of people,"
you said, recalling the country lives we once led.

Yes, I remembered how they used to make merry
under our crab-apple tree when the fruit lay fallen
with that sweet half-rotten smell
just outside the window where we used to
sleep and look out by moonlight;
odor of skunk and apple
alive still stored in our brain cells.

"Thirty years ago. I haven't been this way
for over thirty years."

Appalled I felt the choking bite of Eve's apple
stuck in my throat.
Thirty years from *now* we would be more than ninety
and what then of today?
My running thoughts stopped stock still.

Never to see this road now building finished,
this renewed forest
come to its second prime?

Or perhaps all this wiped out
Hills silent rivers stifled in warm ash
a careless doom dropped
Then a beginning all over?

Not to remember
how we poured hot coffee from the thermos
on this autumn afternoon under a pine tree
while we watched the white dog
smelling and sniffing invisible patterns through the wet grass
Not knowing that time must end?

"How it was thirty years ago in this place."

Here and there ghosts of ourselves cried out of the mirror,
rose to the murmur of water where marvel of marvels
you first showed me the stream that bubbled out of a bare rock
naming it "Moses' Spring."

And where we looked at a mountain
we climbed once together and saw how high it still was
higher even than we had remembered
how tired at the end of that day we still felt
and drank tea in the rainy tent
and slept then
as never since so deep.

It began to grow dark as we drove
chilling me with forewarning of the year's end.
"Night *falls*," you said,
"It really falls in these canyons."
A pause—
"And yet the day *springs*."

A Poem Not Especially in Praise of Cats

Women hate mice but they love a cat.
Tell me, pray, the reason for that.
Mice steal crumbs from the household store
A cat is fed and he screams for more;
more fish, more liver, more round steak ground,
cream by the gallon, meat by the pound.
Horses eat oats and a helping of hay.
Dogs are fed only once a day,
but a cat must eat from morn till night
and then goes hunting till broad daylight.
What does he do with it? Where does it go?
That is a thing I'd be glad to know.
It's not that he's so peripatetic
unless his dreaming is energetic,
for he sleeps all day on the housewife's bed
and grudges her space to lay her head.
He's dead to the world and he will not stir
for the edict of king or of dictat*er*,
but if he hears a sound in the kitchin
he flies to the scene more quick than a witch 'n'
pleads and cries in a pitiful voice
till you'd wring his neck if you had any choice.
Instead you give him, you don't know why,
milk in a bowl and a plate heaped high,
for Kitty must have his frequent dinner
though you and the household all grow thinner.
You say that he pays you back for that
by ridding your house of mouse and rat
but if on this subject you should think twice
perhaps you'd come to prefer the mice.
For mice never bother you to feed them.
They help themselves to things as they need them,
and they can keep quite fat and sleek

for a year on what Kitty would eat in a week.
They build their nests all warm and snug
of fluff from the blanket and fuzz from the rug,
and this may cause you some pain and horror;
still they *don't* have kittens in the bureau drawerer
and they don't wear your nerves as sharp as a pin
by wanting Out and then wanting In.
My own has never yet done what was bid of him
Yet how well he knows I'd never get rid of him!

1940

You Name It

I sat one night up reading late
to find how apes do brachiate.
It wracked my brain and furled my brow
to picture to myself just how
or what the ape was up to when
he started out and came again
from place to place,
from tree to trees
with casual brachiatious ease.

It was a word I did not know
so to some resource I must go.
I asked my boss; I asked my mate,
"Pray tell me how you brachiate?"
The one just gave a solemn nod
and lectured on the brachopod.
The other's arms around me threw
as though he thought I really knew.

But neither answer gave me ease
for brachiopods don't live in trees
and what the apes were said to do
was not described as needing two.
From west to east, from south to north
they *all* went brachiating forth.
One couldn't help be fascinated
at how those great apes brachiated!

At last I wandered to a zoo
and told the head ape, "Howdy do?
I mean, How *do* you brachiate?"
He looked at me and scratched his . . . wait!
You guess the word; it rhymes with ate,

and plate and slate and captivate,
expectorate, congratulate,
hate, Kate and accommodate.

The story's almost done, you see:
He scratched then reached up for his tree
and there did brachiate for me.
(No, this is not pornography.)
From limb to limb he nimbly goes
by both strong, hairy brachios.
So thus I learned that unlike man
the ape is no pedestrian,

And I, who at my age could never brachiate
my weary, plodding homeward way must ambulate.

1964

Chama

The arrogant river
in haste is tearing the world down,
ripping its chasms
downtime,
ruthless, uprooting,
hurling debris of mountains,
a furious housewife
stirring everything up, a woman
who is tired of peace in her house,
who will have creation,
everything out of its place,
rearranged again in any pattern
so long as it is a new one.

Let her alone
Let her alone till she calms down,
till the river is placid and ripples over the rinsed stones,
as innocent now as a woman
who combs her hair,
combs creation out of her long hair.
The fish come gliding,
the water snake is a loosed swirl,
pollywogs unravel.
She combs slowly and forever
as though time meant nothing to her.

1967

On Seeing the Wild Geese

The wild geese
flew south again
toward the end of October.
Some vigilant angel
contrived to get us to the place on time
in spite of the logical plans we'd thought
we were making
to go somewhere else that day.

Dangling a lunch at our shoulders,
the white dog nudging us along,
we were turned back every which way
from where we first tried to go.
All roads seemed blocked but one.

The angel lured us
with a promise of cottonwoods,
their leaves still golden,
along the stream in Santa Clara Canyon
not too far above the Pueblo—
three miles or less—
but it was enough to step clear out of
the noise of our world
that seemed to be rushing with jet speed
toward its own destruction.

The canyon was wide;
its walls were sediments
made out of more than one range
of torn down mountains.
It opened eastward
on the Rio Grande valley
where the earth rises out of a trough

141

like an immense wave
snowcapped and blue at its crest.
The rising and falling
motion
surged through us also
almost as when we were children
the terror and joy within us
of the pushed swing looping upward
away from level earth.

To the west
through the wedge of the steepened canyon
we could see the long line of Tschicoma mountain
lift skyward
calm as a woman's shoulder;
from there the stream rushes down in summer
that waters the Indian fields,
fed now by a mid-autumn rain
running a little too wide to be easily stepped over
in a bed of sand and furious washed gravel.
The gravel bed was covered
with acres of the golden-green shrub
we call chamisa.

Here and there were islands of cottonwood,
old trees, well-spaced, with heavy limbs and branches,
leaves responding to no color
but blazing gold at this season
as though to give the sun itself
back to itself transfigured.
There was a faint odor,
under the trees, of dung
where cattle had rested in the shade on hot noons,
switching flies with their smoothed rope tails.
Our angel bided his own time.

We lunched on chicken and sherry
while the white dog waded the stream or sat
exploring autumn with her moist nose.
It was wonderful
to be alive and to be alone
enough to hear the silence.
The stream was singing with a child's voice
that has not yet learned speech.
We lay still so long we
began to be tuned to the sound of water,
the way the smooth stones were.
At length the white dog
—or was it the angel?—stirred us
out of our mindless daze.
My feet began
to itch, as their habit is.

I wandered off then
in my own way,
leaving you to your own,
so much more content with being
still in one place and time.

The dog and I were goalless,
meandering
here and there, as who knows what spirits
moved us,
she swerving on unknown scents
along the moist sands,
I beckoned by golden leaves or
a rosier seed plume
or the urge like a hunger
to know what secret was waiting
only around the next bend.
I could feel the primitive being

who dreams in us all begin to stir within me,
eyes, ears, skin-senses alert to
the slope of landscape, the
rustle of leaf and water, the
mellow crisp of air.
On the one hand the delicate water
was eating the cliff away;
on the other the golden
leaves kept on slowly falling
free from the tree forever
to their own doom.

1969

May 9, 1977

Falling in love with a purple petunia
the three cut stems and the green leaves;
the full flower like a dancer's
upside down tu-tu; the ruffled petals,
plum-colored with the light coming through them,
the luminous creases,
the pale green secret center,
the dark green head of the pistal
lordly among three delicate arching stamens,
the scent fills the whole room,
the wind and cinnamon scent of a purple petunia
invades my whole being;
a dream of bees, of night moths with their furred wings,
    their feathered antennae.
I am on the verge of changing
into something bewilderingly not human,
a page from the metamorphoses of Ovid,
those girls attacked by a disguised god. . . .

May 14, 1977

The white lilac against the grey evening
is a candelabrum with a thousand tapers;
it is a tree on which a thousand white birds
have suddenly alighted;
it is the white froth on a steep wave;
it is a many-fingered goddess;
it is a cavern in which a mystery is enacted;
it is a branch of slow music.
Suddenly the wind sets every twig in motion;
a ballet of white dancers
leaps out of the green leaves
toward the leaning grey cloud.

In Terms of Water

1.

To tell about a life in terms of water.
As though all one's life had been
following a river
upstream and toward the source.
Or are we the bed of our life's river,
its jagged or sandy opposition?

2.

The world, the world we try to live in,
would be nothing without rivers.
Rivers begin with rain,
sea water rising,
the sun, the energy of light transforming
the visible, invisible
dancing of many waters.

Water taking the form of snow.
Mountains of transfiguration.

3.

The child wondering,
watching the raindrops
merge across the window.
The month old puppy
lifts her head to taste the flying snowflakes.

4.

Born beside the slow flowing Mora
a flood stormed down, extreme and Biblical
in the tenth month of the child's life
before there were words to remember.

Carried to safety,
the young mother, the child, the father
shivered in straw all night
among the tame animals,
the surge of threatening waters.

All their possessions gone
but the scant nightwear they happened to be wearing,
far less warning than Noah
to choose what they might save.

It became a legend in the child's life,
how mother and father
beat the storm back,
beat terror down with laughter.

At daybreak
along the soaked roads
wagons and horses passed them,
bearing the stark drowned.

The mother, scarcely grown yet
out of her indulged girlhood,
sat soldier straight and slight beside her husband
on the harsh ride to rescue.

Her eyes that looked out on death
were cold and scornful. The weaned child slept
on the strong knees of its father.

> There is a history keeps running through
> our human lives
> that binds us beyond time.
> What is it in us that remembers?

The sound of the Mora
blends with Noah's waters.
The ark that bears the living
moves within us.

5.

The Bible runs with rivers,
the presence of still waters.
"The spirit of God moved on the face of the waters.
He drew me forth out of many waters."

"And coming up out of the water he beheld the heavens opened."

There is a river
the waters of which make glad
the city of God,
but that is a world, I think,
none has ever come to
or seen in his living flesh.

6.

Each of us walks through life
by his own river
discovering all its features
like an explorer for the first time.
None has ever traveled
precisely this way before him.

7.

Meriwether Lewis
came to the Great Falls of the Missouri
and wrote in his journal of
their beauty.

". . . the spray dissipated into a thousand shapes
on all of which the sun disperses
the brightest colours of the rainbow.

". . . crossing the point of a hill
for a few hundred yards
he saw one of the most beautiful objects in nature:
the whole Missouri
suddenly stopped by one shelving rock
. . . stretching itself
from one side of the river to another
for at least a
quarter of a mile . . .
For ninety or a hundred yards from the left cliff
the water falls in one smooth even sheet
over a precipice of at least eighty feet.
. . . being received as it falls by the irregular . . . rocks below
it forms a prospect of perfectly white foam . . .
on which the sun impresses the brightest colors
of the rainbow."*

8.

The horror lives in me still—
the white moon's arid waste,
a valley of rocks like dry bones
of a planet
into which not even a poet
would be able to breathe life.

9.

Even the Navaho
in their bare blown wilderness
dreamed of White Shell Woman.

(How I long for words to come
accurate as though chipped out of granite.
They come diffused, amorphous,
shifting as amoeba on a glass slide.)

10.

Last night we talked at dinner
about the motion of snakes,
the tracks they leave
twisting across sand,
the way they glide through water
and over bare land as though they had been poured out.

There are hieroglyphs on our rocks,
a plumed snake.
Far down I watch the river
flow sinuous between black rocks.
Whose ancient eye looks through me.

11.

To whom do I long to speak of water?
Who will ever have ears to listen?
Soon only the dead,
only those who have talked with the old ones
will understand this language.

12.

Anahita,
Goddess of the waters
forgotten by our kind.
What wilderness do you still inhabit?
In what mineral cavern
deep under crusted earth
do you now lie dreaming?

13.

"In the round Zion of the water bead," said Dylan Thomas.
These words haunt me
as though the Presence were suddenly everywhere
in water.

14.

I drink:
It is a rite, a true communion.
Each cup is a chalice.
Suddenly all vessels become Grails.
Even the despised and battered
enamel cup by the edge of the stagnant puddle
at Pine Springs I saw last summer—
all that was left of the rimmed pool
where clear water used to drip
far back in my childhood time.
Even that scorned cup
is all at once transfigured.

15.

When I rise from the toilet
light reflects from the surface of mingled urine
and clear water.
I pull the handle;
the water gushes to flush it,
obedient water
not flinching at the meanest service.

16.

I see St. Francis
kneeling to wash the feet of lepers;
before him the man of Nazareth.
A lesson in the virtue of humility, we called it,
rather puffing ourselves up.
I think he and the woman
who bathed his feet with her tears understood it
in a rather different way.

17.

My father gave me
a sensation of delighted terror

when he tossed me in his strong arms
and let the world drop out beneath me,
never once failing to catch me.
Never quite letting me drop on the hard earth.

And so I grew up fearing ladders and bridges,
dreaming at night of falling, falling
down bottomless sharp vistas.
How I envied the birds whose tethered wings sustained them
on the steep slopes of the bright air.

My father gave me an eye for wide horizons;
my mother an eye for the comfortable enclosed room.
"I never liked windows with views," she said.
She planted shrubbery all around the house walls
and trees in thickets that would not let her see out.

My father gave me a fast horse and let me gallop
to the edges of everywhere, to the edge of clouds and mountains.
My mother gave me a needle and taught me how to thread it
and how to sew in little measured stitches.
From her I learned to fit intricate shapes together,
at least until my father's ghost comes tramping,
slamming doors behind him,
and letting the untethered winds in.

My father gave me a lake with leaping fish in it,
the fisherman's passion
for walking in silence among brush and boulders,
spying deep into this other element
or waiting hours and silently at the edge of light-brazed water
for the sudden tug at the line and the hook taken.

18.
Growing up in an arid landscape
I have learned to know water as a treasure;

153

lain prone to drink it
by the edge of a mountain stream;
dug in moist sand so my sweating horse
could thrust her nose in,
hoed dry earth into channels around my roots.

Like my own mother have brought water
to fevered children,
cool water over dry lips,
the taste of rivers
that once flowed clean out of
repeated Edens.

Water
pools of it in lichened granite
where I have watched my dog lap
and then look up as though she thought I'd made it.

19.
(St. Exupery's Arab
is an ikon of the Saviour.)

20.
I have inhabited
the Biblical wilderness,
known in my own flesh
dryness, the sun burning
over naked, tormented sand.

Dryness. No wonder it became a saint's word.

But also a poet's word.

Poetry,
a bubbling up from who knows
what far depths?

Water that whispers
and sings
its twining rhythms
over and over,
and never entirely the same tune,
over and over, like Bach's aria,
the strands of a Benedictus.

21.
The blow of a horse's hoof
struck moon-shaped Hippocrene
for the muses on a mountain.
I can believe it.
A shod hoof
more than once made its mark
in childhood on my bare flesh.

Pain, and the sudden crying.

This is the way that poetry
often spurts out.

But the deep waters
are seldom touched anymore.
They say that Pegasus
hauls thunderbolts for Zeus like any packhorse.
The harp hangs on the willow
and we are all in exile.

(This series day after day in April, 1970)

* Meriwether, Lewis. *The Journals of Lewis and Clark*. Boston: Houghton
  Mifflin, 1953.

The Truchas Peaks
(Prometheus)

They might have chained Prometheus to this rock:
Twelve thousand feet above the dreamy world,
A gaunt grey crag. The stern relentless wind
Had lashed the twisted trees into retreat
And hurled them down. Only a frail blue flower,
Blue as forget-me-nots, creeps pityingly
Among the rocks.

The dim horizon melts into the sky
And in its arms the beauty of the world
Mocks the proud mountain's stern reality.
They might have chained Prometheus to this rock;
That far off beauty would have gnawed his soul
As some fierce vulture. Not to hear a sound
Save for the beating of a maddened wind
Against the crag, the scream of preying birds;
To watch in vain the glamor of the sun
On the great sea of shadow-painted hills;
This would be pain to him.
And yet, strong-souled,
He might endure all utter loneliness,
All silence and all longing for the world,
For love and laughter and the warmth of song,
All things save this: the pity of the flower,
Blue as forget-me-nots, beneath his feet.

1923

Little Sermon in Stone

The little hill, breast round and hard as stone,
peopled with stones, with dark red stones like blood;
with fist-big stones, and smaller child's hand stones,
seemed at one glance earth's very cinder patch,
infertile, inhospitable to life.
But we stayed there one winter afternoon
hushing our man-proud thought, and stilled our hearts
to the slow beat of time's heart in a stone.

We lay upon the ground and felt the stones,
and saw them with our hands; and with our eyes
tuned to chill light's minute and fragile pulse,
gazed deep into the structure of the stone.
We saw the crystalline flowering of the stone,
the many-faceted complexity,
the light turned back with orchestrated beat
into our listening eyes, the blood stained reds,
the flush of yellow and the dove-dark greens.

We touched this little fragment of a world
burst from earth's straining heart, this ancient rain
that starred the black night once with splintered fire,
and dared the sky to weep till the sky wept
and the rain's fingers quelled the angry light.
This hill became the rounded grave of fire,
ash-cold and ruinous and for an age,
who knows how long, lay obdurate to rain,
all light transfixed and frozen in its heart.

But as we lay
face down, eye close to stone, heart close to stone
we saw the stain of life upon the stones.
The creeping lichens, live and unafraid,

fed upon crystal and transformed the shape
of arrogant rock to supple, pliant dust
and flowered upon that dust. Light became leaf,
and leaf, with who knows what of agony,
contrived its seed to float upon the wind.
The colored lichens take the world apart
in their slow fingers. The bright mold of life
moves like a web upon the unliving rock
and seeks the imprisoned light and sets it free
to live again in seed and stem and flower.

Upon the little hill the frozen grass
stands yellow in the sun. The winter birds
pause and are fed. We too were fed
through mind and heart upon stone's element.

                                        1940

Wilderness Experience

I wept to find man's heart so hard.
Against my own heart's stone I wept
to know my heart was hard as man's.
In wilderness I walked and cried
for power to turn these stones to bread
that all men's children might be fed.
Why must man's heart, I asked, be hard?

And then upon one hard white stone
I saw that something lived and bloomed,
a brave green stain upon the stone,
nor wept because the stone was hard,
nor even that the lily's root
wove of more supple dust its fruit.

Shall man be less than this, I said,
whose life lies not in bread alone?
Shall God not bloom upon the heart
as even on the stubborn stone?
I marveled at the sudden trace
of mercy on my brother's face.

1949

Theme and Cogitations

He said, "It is *your* feeling that you give the stone."
I gnaw on this thought like a dog with a juicy bone.
But how, whence, why do I give it? Where is it gone
when I have given it? This stone lay on the shore
a day, a year, maybe a hundred years or more,
and before that how many millions ago was it a mountain?
And before that maybe a magma, a molten fountain
deep in the earth's crust, and before that a jet of terrible light
seething out of the sun. And where was I, I wonder—
this little dot of consciousness called I
that now after all these milleniums happens to stand
by the sea and takes this particular stone in her hand
and feels it grow warm and feels time under her finger
like the pulse at a flesh and blood wrist, and sees the nebulae whirl
in spiralling rose and blue and the heavens unfurl
with every line a diagram of space and all that moves there?
How abstract is the stone! Why does my heart quicken
and somethng rise in my throat like tears?
Something that wants to waken
that sleeps in the stone and dreams of being human.

1956

Controversy

Taking a small stone in her hand, she said:
"God's very word is written in this stone,
and who will ask that it be changed to bread?"

He said, "Man does not live by bread alone;
but without bread he does not even live.
What comfort could a stone or God's word give?"

"Have you not seen," she asked, "that men can die
before whose very mouths bread stands heaped high,
or living bodies harboring a dead soul
which only by God's word could be made whole?"

"But to be whole and have no bread," said he,
"is only mystical nonsensity.
Men cry for bread, and you who hear their groans
assist their murder when you offer stones."

"If you could read this stone," she said, "you'd see
the image of your own heart's agony
and know that you and the small stone are one
with every suffering thing beneath the sun,
and that God strives within you and the stone
until you make his deathless form your own.
He who has listened to God's word," she said,
"will share with all that lives his living bread."

"But dead men serve no God," he said. "God's word
above starvation's cry is seldom heard."

"Yet men have starved themselves," said she, "as though a greater hunger could be answered so."

"Still I must fight for men that they have bread.
And I that they be filled with God," she said.

1942

Still Life

A round plate on the breakfast table
holds in its white circumference
four colored stones,
a handful of sand dollars,
a twisted root washed up by the formless ocean.

Each morning she plays with them a little
like a child throwing jacks:
the mineral colors of the stones,
the rough sea-creatures,
the blind root shaped like something not yet human.

She cannot let them lie.
She cannot see the stones as only stones.
She says, "If these were birds and they could fly!"
and suddenly the air is full of birds;
the colors move and sing.

Sand dollars are sea urchins,
urchins, echinoderms are spiny skins,
the words are horror's kin.
Her hair stands up
prickled with ancient dread.

There is a creature struggling in the root
to free itself.
Its voiceless agony
draws all her muscles taut.
Morning upon new morning brings no change.
The birds fly back into their stones again.

1958

163

Among the Holy Stones

The world I moved through
all day
seemed as much inside me
as it did all around.

Shakespeare's "delighted spirit"
got mixed with Blake's bird,
that "vast universe of delight" our senses
most often keep closed out.

These were
once fiery New Mexico mountains we walked on.
Inside, a mountain of transfiguration
became their reflection.

"In your own Bosom you bear your heaven
and Earth and all you behold."

We drank our thermos coffee on a hillside
among the holy stones.

1965

(Untitled)

Poems ache
in the heart
the way stones do
in our abdominal organs;
stones
that must travel a rough way
to excretion, tearing tissue,
sometimes no exit;
a mineral convexity
is wedged firm
in the constricted channel;
nothing issues
forth except now and then
a mute tear.

1975

She Will Want Nothing But Stones

The time coming,
is soon here
when she will want nothing
but stones;
to live among them
on a barren hillside,
angled or round with fragments,
crystal facets
in which the light plays
luminous metaphors:

congealed rain,
mineral reflections
of sunrise and sunset
colors.

One afternoon
she lay there
among the slanting rays of winter,
caught in the golden vase of autumn;
the sandhill cranes flew over
invisible as angels;
their cries fell
in a shower of shaken petals;
the thin air echoed
like wand-struck bells made of crystal.

"Perhaps I shall take root here like the pines"
she had written long ago
in the beginning of this marriage.
Today aware only of bone,
nothing but bone left

among the stones,
the fossil imprint
all that remained now
of what had once been human.

1974

The Kites and the Petroglyphs

A medley of children
and a melody of kites
on this February afternoon.
The air
a hemisphere of light blue,
radiant light;
the kites streamed in it
like tadpoles in a millpond,
slender and serpentine,
colored rose-red,
colored purple;
one butterfly fluttering;
one with a little tail that twinkled
like a caught star dipped in silver.

It seemed like an odd place to fly kites—
thirty miles more or less from anywhere,
at the tip of a blunt-finned ridge of lava
cutting the cliff-rimmed plain in two.
We had to crawl through
a tight-pulled, barbed-wire fence to get there,
meant to keep cattle in and intruders out.
We knew we were trespassing but
the place had been ceremonial
long before cattle and fences.
Ancient holy beings were glyphed onto the smooth rock;
sky beings had been invoked with power here.

I wondered if we had perhaps been summoned
by spirits tired of long sleeping, to hold our feast among them,
a little festival of stringed kites
that looped and spun in the bright air.
Among their stars and serpents

we sent our own.
We became children with our children
for the space of an afternoon,
fulfilled, filled full of light.
The ancint Beings
seemed to laugh with us.
Old Kokopelli
hunched on his rock,
lifted his fertile flute
and smiled too.

1977

Basalt Dike with Petroglyphs

1.

We walked this bony ridge
in mid-October:
midday,
imagining midnight;
planets marching
bright as the shield of heroes;
imagined the sun's rising,
its light broken like water by a sharp reef,
the spinal remnant of a beached sea-creature
crawled up on land
in an age far from ours,
stretching its length along it
to die at last of too much aspiration,
of milleniums of sunlight.

2.

Hunters of ancient time
pondered upon it
awed at this arrowed axis,
these slabs of smoothed rock
from which, at the top of the ridge,
all earth seemed sky;
drew suns and stars on the vertical surfaces,
horned and masked figures
from lost mythologies,
a bird-headed shaman,
erect serpents, spirals;
symbols that spoke to us,
to something that listened in our blood.
We were untaught children
reading a picture book,
its single pages scattered on the slope

like eggs hidden at Easter.
Come see! Come see! we cried to one another
while invisible presences smiled beyond time to hear us.

3.

What artist hand drew eagle-headed figures
on these blind stones?
small earthy animals, birds,
cloud terraces, trees,
strong pawprint of a bear,
an eagle's claw,
then, balancing nature, drew his own left hand,
completion and testament.

4.

We gazed on a seasonal world, a zodiac
in astonished recognition,
circled like ours
and centered.
The east-west axis
of day and night,
winter and summer
in alternate revolution.
These barren, wind-swept ledges
were sealed with a ritual
forgotten, yet familiar;
the rocks were alive with being.
The ridge we walked on was a compass arrow
aimed toward the planet's rising.

5.

Entranced with sun and air
we lay for a time on the sloping tip of the landmark
as though on a ship's prow.
The tidal movements
within the earth swept through us,

invisible forces
that marry earth to sky.
Prayers had been imprinted
long ago on these silent stones,
incised like music
upon mute surfaces.
We lay while our hearts listened.
Was it the wind we heard
or the hump-backed flute player
among the hidden rocks?
A sound of dancers
wove earth and sky into a single blessing.

1976

Stones on an Arid Hillside

Stones that lie scattered on an arid hillside
longing for beauty in the eye of the beholder;
there are rainbows in them
waiting for definition,
dance figures, ritual intentions.

A stone cannot move by itself
yet something in it delights in motion,
to roll down a steep slope,
to be carried somewhere by water,
to emigrate in great companies as birds do.

Perhaps stones are a motion picture
slowed down to the point of immobility.
If the film could be speeded up
what a tremendous onrush:
a stampede of stones hurling themselves toward ocean
dragging rivers along behind them.

Stones only seem motionless
because my mind cannot keep up with their gyrations.
If I hold one long enough
the atoms will start whirling;
the cold stone warms;
I feel it throb in my hand like a caught bird or a secret.

"God's activity is not the same in a man as in a stone,"
said Meister Eckhart.
I tremble to think of the god's activity,
the lines of force that meet here,
earth's weight, the moon's rhythmical attraction;
the essence of time compacted in such small mass.
The stone is not mortal yet there is a spirit in it;

it absorbs light.
When it becomes dust it too will some day feed roots.

"When attention is directed to the idea of a stone
the idea of an angel cannot be entertained."
These words of Eckhart's
prick at my slow mind.
I find I cannot think of one without the other.
A stone is more enigmatic than an angel.
I ask it questions;
it answers me in riddles.
I read it like the palm of my hand.
What if it were a fragment of a god's hand,
a fingerprint, undeniable evidence?
Among thousands and thousands
how long will it be before I find the right one?

I keep thinking the markings in stones
are like grooves of music
that could be played if only I knew how,
if only I had the right instrument,
the correct equation,
a sense more compatible than my stale ear.
Suppose each stone were packed full of sound
as a computer's memory—
If I pressed the right key
would I hear the crystals growing?
Would colors be audible?
Would the stones call out to one another,
each sounding its own note like a deep bell?
If I could learn how to listen
would I someday hear the stone's voice
that goes on and on putting God into its own words?

An Afternoon among Stones

1.

It is terrible to be so moved by a mere stone
on its remnant of riverbank from a past age;
a white stone as round as a kneecap or a child's skull,
not so much white as mooncolor,
not so much round as oval;
a marvel of substance, of hardness
that time alone could mold,
time and the thrust of a long-vanished river,
torrents of water rolling it over and over
the way we children once rolled clay between our curved palms.

2.

My heart stops to think how stones are always in the making
that seem to lie about so quiet and speechless
in the bed of dry arroyos.
They form patterns like the handfuls of jacks we used to play with,
sorting themselves into numbers,
becoming threes, fifteens or sixes,
playing Still Pond No More Moving
until the fierce disorder of the next storm frees them
once more into motion, rolling them on and onward,
grinding them against one another,
abrading them with sand grains,
flinging them loose once more at random
like a spilled alphabet,
clusters of words to be read like an oracle.

3.

You said as we started our walk inside the crystal
of that October afternoon,
"I have always thought this place is really heaven."
So I too found it.

This was the miracle: the two of us were witness
to the same transubstantiation,
the ripplemarks in the sand, the cliff shapes echoed
in the low sandy borders of the arroyo,
the individual beauty of each strewn stone
as though each contained an angel.

4.

This moon-white stone
was inscribed along its brow with a cryptic writing
like a musical notation,
a message that seemed to speak, not to our learning
but to a wisdom in us like the stone's
that we read without knowing how we read.
I grope for words to translate but I cannot.
The meaning is felt, not read.
There is a god in this stone or something like one.
Within us there is something like a god that answers.

5.

Kneeling we laid our hands on the warm stone and listened,
touching the stone in a mutual benediction.
Human and mortal as we were, the mute stone blessed us
and absorbed from us our blessing;
its angel and ours touched hands.
I heard—did you hear?—the sound of an ancient river
and the cry of great birds in migration passing over.

1979

Sandhill Cranes in February

And on and on they came
through the pale afternoon,
long strands and ribbons,
arcs and curving wedges,
hieroglyphs in motion,
staves of music.

We looked upward again and again and saw them flying
and as they flew they called to one another;
the call sounded
through those myriad throats like the voice of a single being
half-angel and half-bird,
a wind sound, a water sound,
a sound as golden as honey.
We listened and felt ourselves enchanted
beyond our mortal sense.

All afternoon the sky was our dancing ground.
The long song rose and fell.
The convergent lines formed circles.
We were children again in ring around a rosy
immersed in a mystery.
In the end we must all fall down
and down in a slow spiral out of heaven
and be ourselves again.

Earth and our stolid bodies claimed us.
We leaned against stones.
The white clouds were slate clean.
On either side the cliffs were voiceless sandstone.
All afternoon the cranes kept flying over
aligning themselves with music.

As the sound ebbed we spoke wistfully of dying,
when our time came, into such ecstasy.

1981

Appendix

Some of the poems appearing in this book are from previously published volumes, as follows:

from the published works:

from *Foretaste* (1933):
After Looking into a
   Genealogy
Do Not Feel Sure
Shadow-Madness
Bridal
Evergreen
I Have Looked at the Earth
Foretaste
Peach Trees

**from *Familiar Journey*
   (1936):**
On a Morning
And There Was Light
East of the Sun and West of
   the Moon
After the Rain
This Ocean (Point Lobos)
Familiar Journey
Enchanted Mesa
Autumn Dusk

**from *Ultimatum for Man*
   (1946):**
Poem to Accompany the Gift
   of a Loaf of Bread
School Boy
Omens
Sic Transit Gloria

The Nuclear Physicists
Horses in the Moonlight
Here Is Ground Juniper
Morning on Tseregé

**from *The House at Otowi
   Bridge* (1959):**
The Woman Who Dwells
Tilano of San Ildefonso

**from *New and Selected Poems*
   (1976):**
Peñas Negras
Elegy in Three Movements for
   Alice and Haniel Long
Alas
Elements for an
   Autobiography
Lament
Master Race
Blue Heron

**from *The Ripened Fields*
   (1978):**
The Sonnets: I, IV, V, VIII,
   X, XII, XIII, XIV, XV

**from *Birds of Daybreak*
   (1985):**
Black Mesa: Dream and
   Variations

Bibliography

Church, Peggy Pond. *Birds of Daybreak*. Santa Fe: William Gannon, 1985.

———. *Familiar Journey*. Santa Fe: Writers' Editions, 1936.

———. *Foretaste*. Santa Fe: Writers' Editions, 1933.

———. *The House at Otowi Bridge*. Albuquerque: University of New Mexico Press, 1959.

———. *New and Selected Poems*. Boise: Boise State University, 1976.

———. *The Ripened Fields*. Santa Fe: The Lightning Tree, 1957.

———. *Rustle of Angels*. Denver: Peartree Press, 1981.

———. *Ultimatum for Man*. Stanford: James Ladd Delkin, 1946.

———. *Wind's Trail: The Early Life of Mary Austin*. Santa Fe: Museum of New Mexico Press, 1990.

Coles, Robert. *Eskimos, Chicanos, Indians*. Boston: Little-Brown, 1977.

Fergusson, Erna. *Our Southwest*. New York: Knopf, 1940.

Henderson, Alice Corbin. *The Turquoise Trail*. Boston: Houghton Mifflin, 1928.

Levertov, Denise. *The Poet in the World*. New York: New Directions, 1973.

Long, Haniel. *Interlinear of Cabeza de Vaca*. With an afterword by Peggy Pond Church. Tucson: Peccary Press, 1985.

Lummis, Charles F. *The Land of Poco Tiempo*. Albuquerque: University of New Mexico Press, 1928.

Major, Mabel and T.M. Pearce. *Southwest Heritage*. Albuquerque: University of New Mexico Press, 1938.

Proust, Marcel. *The Past Recaptured*. New York: Random House, 1932.

Rich, Adrienne. *Adrienne Rich's Poetry*. Edited by Barbara Charles Worth Gelpi and Albert Gelpi. New York: Norton, 1975.

Sarton, May. Letters in Peggy Pond Church's Collection, 1951–1985.

Thoreau, Henry David. *Journals*. Boston: Houghton Mifflin, 1927.

Welty, Eudora. "Place in Fiction." *South Atlantic Quarterly 55*, 1956.

Wilhelm, Richard (translator). *The Secret of the Golden Flower: A Chinese Book of Life*. New York: Harcourt Brace Jovanovich, 1962.

THE RED CRANE LITERATURE SERIES

Dancing to Pay the Light Bill:
Essays on New Mexico and the Southwest by Jim Sagel

Death in the Rain, a novel by Ruth Almog

The Death of Bernadette Lefthand, a novel by Ron Querry

Stay Awhile: A New Mexico Sojourn, essays by Toby Smith

This Dancing Ground of Sky: The Selected Poetry of
Peggy Pond Church by Peggy Pond Church

Working in the Dark: Reflections of a Poet of the Barrio,
writings by Jimmy Santiago Baca